Leaving Certificate
Biology
Experiment Book

3rd Edition

Joe Rice · Siobhán Kirwan

The Educational Company of Ireland

First published 2013
The Educational Company of Ireland
Ballymount Road
Walkinstown
Dublin 12
www.edco.ie

A member of the Smurfit Kappa Group plc

ISBN 978–1–84536–555–4

Editor: Jane Rogers
Design and Layout: Identikit
Proofreader: Penelope Lyons
Cover Design: One House Design, Identikit
Illustrations: Daghda

Photograph Acknowledgements
Alamy, Science Photo Library, Shutterstock

Web references in this book are intended as a guide for teachers. At the time of going to press, all web addresses were active and contained information relevant to the topics in this book. However, The Educational Company of Ireland and the authors do not accept responsibility for the views or information contained on these websites. Content and addresses may change beyond our control and pupils should be supervised when investigating websites.

Introduction

This workbook contains a series of instructions on how to carry out the mandatory practical activities prescribed by the Department of Education and Skills in the Leaving Certificate Biology Syllabus.

At the end of each activity, there is a selection of questions designed to test the student's knowledge of the practical activity they have carried out and of a broader range of related material. Some of the questions are specific and some are more general or applied. An excellent knowledge of the practical activities is essential for all students as Section B of the Leaving Certificate Biology exam (both higher and ordinary level) specifically examines the practical part of the course. Section B is worth 60 marks (15% of the total marks available). Each year to date, practical questions have also appeared in Sections A and C.

Practical work is an excellent and enjoyable way of investigating and strengthening theory learned in theory classes. However, it must be remembered that practical work is potentially hazardous and students must always be aware of this.

Before each practical class, students should try to identify the risks associated with the activity and determine what can be done to minimise these risks. This should be done through discussion with the class teacher and classmates.

This book contains a list of general laboratory safety rules. It must be remembered that this list is not exhaustive and that any uncertainties should be discussed with the class teacher. It is important that students use the following guidelines while conducting, recording and assessing the experimental procedures.

- Follow all steps in the manual.
- Note the safety measures required.
- Assess the risks involved in carrying out the experiment.
- Outline the procedures followed.
- Draw a diagram of the apparatus used.
- Record results.
- Show the results using graphs/charts.
- Take note of experimental errors that may arise.
- Evaluate results and compare them to theoretical results.
- State new skills attained while carrying out the experiment.
- Finally, list any applications, industrial or otherwise, to which their skills may be applied.

Further information on guidelines can be accessed from the Biology SLSS website at http://biology.slss.ie/laboratoryandfieldwork.html.

How to use this book

Each activity follows this layout:

- **Theory:** An introduction which gives the student a background to the practical activity.
- **Materials:** A list of materials required for the activity.
- **Procedure:** An outline of the procedure to be followed.
- **Student Report:** This is the student's personal log of the activity. The **Student Report** section follows this layout:
  - **Title:** Each activity has a title and also includes a space for writing the date on which the activity was carried out.
  - **Procedure:** The student should outline the procedures they followed in a simple list format.
  - **Results:** While carrying out the activity the student should record his or her initial results here.
  - **Diagram:** Diagrams should be drawn in pencil and labelled.

- **Graph** (where relevant): Show each point clearly and enter units on each graph.
- **Risks:** This section allows the student, and their class and teacher, to identify potential hazards.
- **Risk management:** The student should outline procedures to reduce hazards.
- **Skills:** Note any skills used.
- **Skill application:** Note where these skills can be used.
- **Conclusions/comments:** In this section the student draws their initial conclusion on the activity, explores errors, if any, that occurred during the activity and the reasons why such errors occurred.
- **Signature:** By signing this, the student now has his or her own personal record of the activity.
- **Questions:** These follow-up questions allow the student to test their knowledge of the activity and its theoretical background.

Safety in the Laboratory

These guidelines should be discussed in class with a qualified person before any practical activity is undertaken.

Students may only enter the laboratory in the company of an authorised person. When they are in the laboratory, they must abide by the following procedures and others outlined in individual experiments. Students should **remember at all times that the laboratory is a dangerous environment**. All students should, prior to carrying out any activity, be fully acquainted with their school laboratory safety statement. They should then discuss and agree the safety aspects of the activity with their teacher.

Below are some suggested precautions that a student should follow in the laboratory in conjunction with their school laboratory safety statement.

1. Safety spectacles must be worn at all times.
2. If any chemicals are splashed on a student's clothing or skin, these should be removed immediately with water and reported to the person in charge.
3. If a student swallows or receives a splash to the eye from any reagent, immediately seek assistance.
4. All flammable chemicals should be kept away from naked flames.
5. Extreme care should be exercised when using cutting equipment, e.g. scalpels and blades.
6. All biological material should be disposed of in an appropriate manner.
7. Disposable gloves should be worn when handling microbiological material and blood.
8. No eating in the laboratory.
9. All bags and coats should be left outside the working area. Only notebooks and pens are required.
10. Students should be careful when moving chemicals around the laboratory.
11. All spillages and breakages should be reported immediately.
12. Students with long hair should have it tied up.

The authors and the publisher cannot be held responsible for any negligence in following the experiments in this book.

Table of Contents

Chapter **1** | Qualitative Tests of Food Materials

Theory:

Food is required by the body to give energy, help the body grow and fight disease. To carry out these diverse activities, a variety of foodstuffs is required in a balanced diet. In this series of experiments you are asked to carry out a collection of standard tests to ascertain the presence of the major food groups (i.e. carbohydrates, proteins and fats).

Activity **1a** To test for reducing sugar

Materials:

- Glucose solution (1%)
- Food samples
- Benedict's reagent
- Test tubes
- Test tube rack and holder
- Thermometer
- Water bath
- Mortar and pestle

Procedure:

1. Label 6 test tubes A–F.
2. Place 2cm³ glucose solution in A.
3. Place 2cm³ water (control) in B.
4. Place 2cm³ of each of the other food samples in C–F.
5. Add 2cm³ of Benedict's reagent to each test tube.
6. Place the test tubes in a water bath at 80–100°C for 5–10 minutes.
7. Swirl the test tubes and note any colour changes.
8. Record results in the table below.

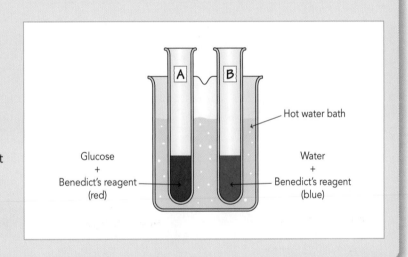

Colour change for positive result: The solution starts blue and turns yellow to brick red depending on the concentration of reducing sugar present.

When using solid food samples: Place about 2g of the sample in a mortar and pestle. Grind the sample. Place the sample in a 100cm³ beaker with 20cm³ of distilled water and heat gently for 5 minutes. Then filter and cool.

Benedict's reagent is a corrosive solution; students should use safety glasses and avoid contact with skin.

Title: _____

_____ *Date:* _____

Procedure:

_____
_____
_____
_____
_____
_____
_____
_____
_____
_____
_____
_____
_____
_____
_____

Results:

Tube	Food	Colour change	Presence/absence of reducing sugar
A	Glucose		
B	Water		
C			
D			
E			
F			

Diagram:

Risks:

Risk management:

Skills:

Skill application:

Conclusions/comments:

Signature:

Activity **1b** To test for starch

Materials:

- Starch solution (1%)
- Food samples
- Iodine solution
- Test tubes
- White tile
- Test tube rack and holder
- Mortar and pestle

Procedure:

1 Label 6 test tubes A–F.
2 Place 2cm³ of starch solution in A.
3 Place 2cm³ of water (control) in B.
4 Place 2cm³ of each of the other food samples in C–F.
5 Add 2–3 drops of iodine solution to each test tube.
6 Swirl the test tubes and note any colour change. (Use a white tile for solid foods.)
7 Record results in the table below.

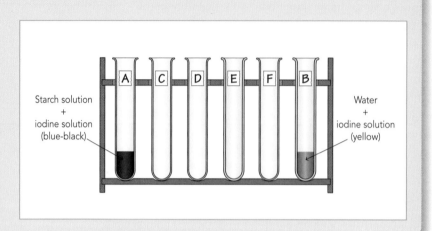

Colour change for positive result: The orange-brown colour of iodine changes to a blue-black colour in the presence of starch.

When using solid food samples: Place about 2g of the sample in a mortar and pestle. Grind the sample. Place the sample in a 100cm³ beaker with 20cm³ of distilled water and heat gently for 5 minutes. Then filter and cool.

STUDENT REPORT **Activity** **1b**

Title: _____

_____ Date: _____

Procedure:

_____
_____
_____
_____
_____
_____
_____
_____
_____

Procedure:

_____

_____

_____

_____

Results:

Tube	Food	Colour change	Presence/absence of starch
A	Starch		
B	Water		
C			
D			
E			
F			

Diagram:

Risks:

Risk management:

Skills:

Skill application:

Conclusions/comments:

Signature:

Activity **1c** To test for fat

Materials:

- Brown paper
- Vegetable oil
- Food samples
- Dropper
- Lamp
- Mortar and pestle

Procedure:

1 Tear the brown paper into 6 pieces and label them A–F.

2 Place 2–3 drops of oil on A.

3 Place 2–3 drops of water (control) on B.

4 Place 2–3 drops of each of the other food samples on C–F.

5 Leave the pieces of paper to dry.

6 Hold each piece of paper to the lamp; note the presence or absence of a permanent translucent stain.

7 Record results in the table below.

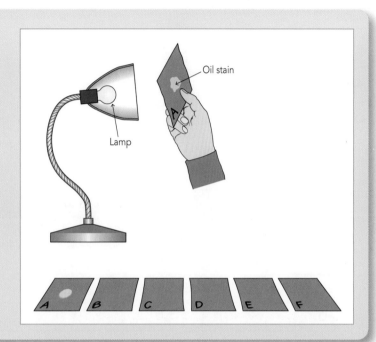

Change for a positive result: A translucent stain from the food sample on the dried brown paper shows the presence of fat.

When using solid food samples: Place about 2g of the sample in a mortar and pestle. Grind the sample. Place the sample in a 100cm^3 beaker with 20cm^3 of distilled water and heat gently for 5 minutes. Then filter and cool.

STUDENT REPORT Activity **1c**

Title: _____

_____ *Date:* _____

Procedure:

_____

_____

_____

_____

_____

Procedure:

_____
_____
_____
_____
_____
_____
_____
_____

Results:

Paper	Food	Colour change	Presence/absence of fat
A	Oil		
B	Water		
C			
D			
E			
F			

Diagram:

Risks:

_____
_____
_____
_____

Risk management:

_____
_____
_____
_____

Skills:

_____
_____
_____
_____

Skill application:

_____
_____
_____
_____

Conclusions/comments:

_____
_____
_____
_____

Signature:

_____

Activity **1d** To test for protein (biuret test)

Materials:

- Milk or egg white
- Food samples
- Sodium hydroxide solution (10%) ⎫
- Copper sulfate solution (1%) ⎭ Biuret reagent

- Test tubes
- Test tube rack and holder
- Mortar and pestle

Procedure:

1 Label 6 test tubes A–F.
2 Put 2cm³ of milk or egg white in test tube A.
3 Place 2cm³ water (control) in B.
4 Place 2cm³ of each of the other food samples in C–F.
5 Add 2cm³ of sodium hydroxide solution and 2–3 drops of copper sulfate solution to each test tube.
6 Swirl the test tube and note any colour change.
7 Record results in the table below.

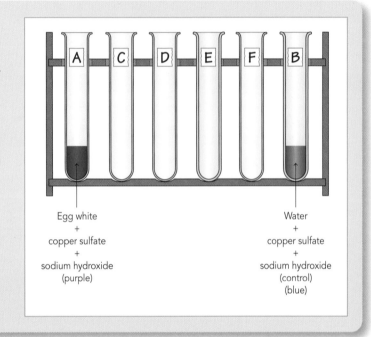

Egg white
+
copper sulfate
+
sodium hydroxide
(purple)

Water
+
copper sulfate
+
sodium hydroxide
(control)
(blue)

Colour change for positive result: The blue solution turns purple in the presence of protein.

When using solid food samples: Place about 2g of the sample in a mortar and pestle. Grind the sample. Place the sample in a 100cm³ beaker with 20cm³ of distilled water and heat gently for 5 minutes. Then filter and cool.

 Biuret reagent is a corrosive solution; students should use safety glasses and avoid contact with skin.

STUDENT REPORT   **Activity**   **1d**

Title: _____

_____   *Date:* _____

Procedure:

_____
_____
_____
_____
_____
_____
_____
_____
_____
_____
_____
_____
_____
_____
_____
_____

Results:

Tube	Food	Colour change	Presence/absence of protein
A	Milk/egg white		
B	Water		
C			
D			
E			
F			

Diagram:

Risks:

_____

_____

_____

Risk management:

_____

_____

_____

Skills:

_____

_____

_____

Skill application:

_____

_____

_____

Conclusions/comments:

_____

_____

_____

Signature:

_____

Activity 1	Questions

1 What control is used when carrying out these food tests?

_____

_____

2 Why are controls used in biological experiments?

_____

_____

3 Name the reagent/s used when testing for:

Reducing sugar _____

Starch _____

Fat _____

Protein _____

4 Complete the table:

Food	Reagent/s	Result
	Iodine	
Reducing sugar	Benedict's reagent	
	Sodium hydroxide and copper sulfate (biuret reagent)	Purple
Fat		Translucent stain

5 Give one function in the body of each of the following:

Protein _____

Fat _____

Sugar _____

Starch _____

6 Name a food that is rich in each of the following:

Protein _____

Fat _____

Sugar _____

Starch _____

7 Write down the elements found in each of the following:

Protein _____

Fat _____

Sugar _____

Starch _____

8 During testing, an apple slice showed a positive result for both starch and reducing sugar. What does this tell you about the apple as a food storage organ?

_____

_____

9 While testing various samples of food for starch, a student noticed different shades of blue-black. What does this tell you about the samples?

_____

_____

10 What result would you expect if a student carried out a Benedict's reagent test on a solution of table sugar (sucrose)? Give a reason for your answer.

_____

_____

11 What chemicals are present in biuret solution?

_____

12 Which food test requires the presence of heat?

_____

Examination note

These activities were examined in Section B of the Leaving Cert Biology Examination in **2012** (OL), **2011** (HL), **2010** (HL), **2009** (OL), **2007** (OL) and **2006** (HL).

They also appeared in Section C **2004** (OL) Q10b, c; and in Section A **2011** (HL) Q1a, **2008** (HL) Q1e, **2006** (OL) Q3 and **2005** (HL) Q1d.

Chapter 2 | Study of an Ecosystem

As part of the Leaving Cert Biology course you are required to carry out some ecology fieldwork. A number of different ecosystems may be studied. You are required to study only one of these ecosystems. The following is a list of possible ecosystems that you could study.

1	Sea shore	**4**	Hedgerow
2	Fresh water pond or canal	**5**	Bog
3	Grassland	**6**	Woodland

This chapter contains a series of worksheets that can be used to record your ecology fieldwork activities. Further information to help you choose an ecosystem and then to identify, estimate numbers and present data of flora and fauna associated with your ecosystem is available at www.edco.ie/lcbiologyexperimentbook.

Fieldwork involves the following steps.

1 Map the habitat.*
2 Collect plants and animals present (Activity 2).
3 Identify plants and animals present (Activity 3).
4 Estimate the number of plants and animals (Activity 4).
5 Measure the environmental (abiotic) factors (Activity 5).
6 Present the information gathered.

* This is not a mandatory activity but is a worthwhile exercise to give you an overview of the ecosystem.

The following is a list of the prescribed Leaving Certificate ecology fieldwork activities.

- ACTIVITY 2 – To use various pieces of apparatus to collect plants and animals in an ecosystem.
- ACTIVITY 3 – To use simple keys to identify any five fauna and any five flora.
- ACTIVITY 4 – To carry out a quantitative study of a habitat.
- ACTIVITY 5 – To investigate three abiotic factors in a selected ecosystem.

Mapping the habitat

Site description

Give a brief description of the area of study. Include answers to some of the following questions.

- What is the name of the area and where is it located?
- Is it exposed or surrounded by walls or cliffs?
- Is it level or not?
- Which way does the site face, e.g. north or south?

_____

_____

_____

_____

_____

Profile map

Draw a profile map if the area of study has a slope (e.g. rocky seashore, hilly land, uneven open ground).

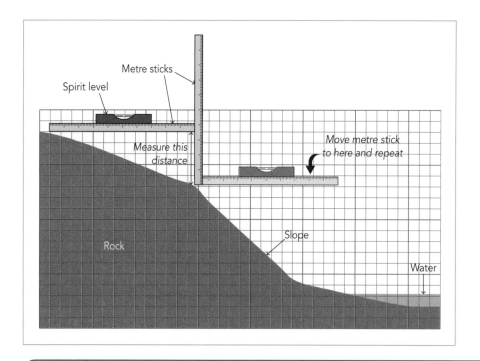

Materials:

- Measuring tape
- Two metre sticks
- Spirit level

Procedure:

1 Tape a spirit level to a metre stick.
2 Place the metre stick horizontally at the top of the slope.
3 Using a second metre stick, measure the distance down to the ground.
4 Move the horizontal metre stick to the base of the vertical stick and repeat the process.
5 Record your readings in the table below.
6 Draw a profile map in the space provided.

Distance down slope	Measurement (m)	Vertical drop from top of slope
1		
2		
3		
4		
5		
6		
7		
8		
9		
10		

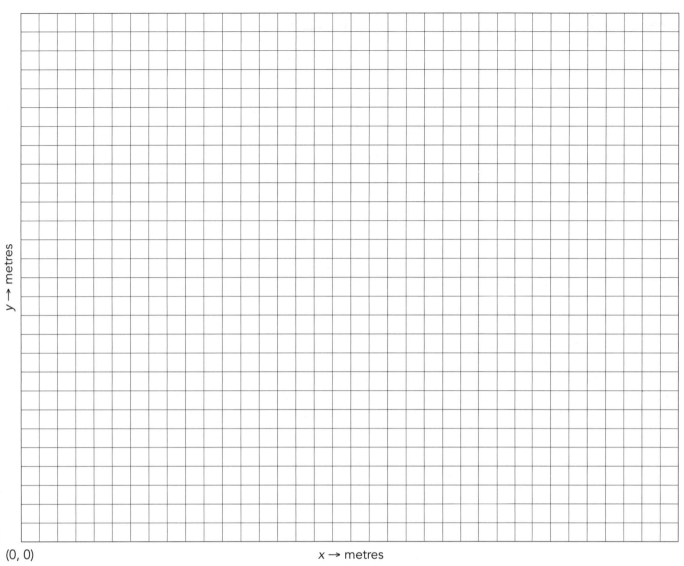

$y \rightarrow$ metres

(0, 0) $x \rightarrow$ metres

Grid reference map

Draw a grid reference map if the area of study is relatively flat and open (e.g. woodland, grassland).

Materials:

- Two lines (30m)
- Stakes (tent pegs)
- Measuring tape

Procedure:

1 Stake two lines (30 metres in length) at right angles to one another.
2 Note a plant/animal you wish to map.
3 Using a measuring tape, measure the distance from each line. Record this in the table provided.
4 Mark the position of the plant/animal on the grid reference map.
5 Repeat this for a number of plants/animals.
6 Also mark on the grid reference map the position of any non-living factors noted (e.g. ponds, streams, walls, paths).

Plant/animal	Position (x,y)

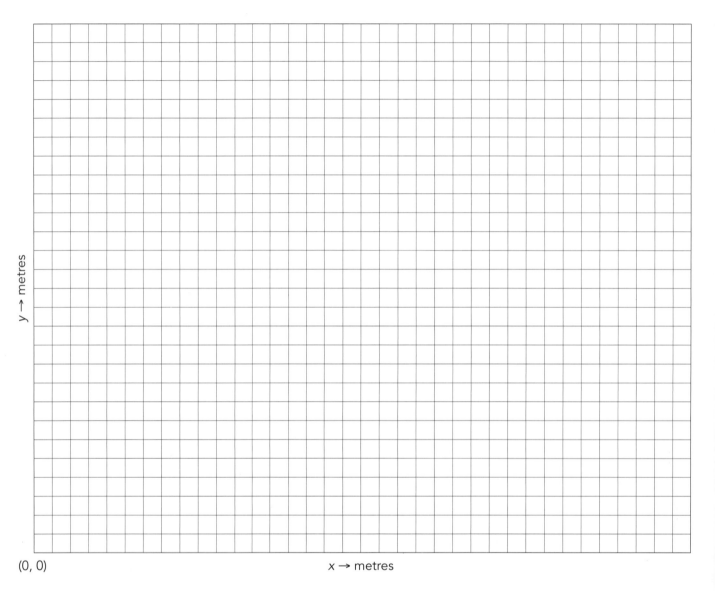

$y \rightarrow$ metres

(0, 0)

$x \rightarrow$ metres

Aspect of the site

The aspect of the site is the direction it faces. The aspect of the site can be considered to be an abiotic factor.

Materials:

- Hand-held compass
- Profile map/grid reference map

Procedure:

1. Stand at the point (0, 0).
2. Hold the compass in your hand and note the location of north on the compass.
3. Mark north on the profile map/grid reference map.

STUDENT REPORT Mapping the habitat

Name/type/description of ecosystem surveyed:

_____

_____

_____

_____

_____

Map/photograph/profile:

Activity 2 — To use various pieces of apparatus to collect plants and animals in an ecosystem

Note: Do not remove any of the collected species from the habitat. Where possible, return all plants and animals to their original location. Leave the site as you found it. Beware of dangers (e.g. deep water, stinging plants, slippery surfaces, steep inclines, etc.). Obtain permission from the owner before entering private property.

Materials:

Collection equipment	Suggested locations for use
Plastic bags	All
Basins	All
Bottles	All
Forceps	All
Knife	All
Spade	All
Labels	All
Scissors	All
Washing-up liquid bottles	Soil
Fish net	Ponds, rock pools, seashore
Insect nets	Woodland, hedgerow, grassland
Plankton net	Seashore
Mammal trap	Woodland, hedgerow, bog, grassland
Beating tray	Woodland, hedgerow
Tullgren funnel	Woodland, hedgerow
Pooter	Woodland, hedgerow
Pit-fall trap	Woodland, hedgerow, grassland

Plankton net

Mammal trap

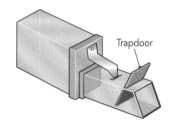

Beating tray

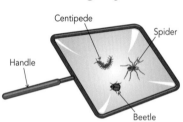

Pooter

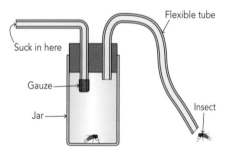

Pit-fall trap

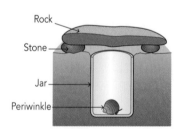

Tullgren funnel

Procedure:

1 Choose the items from the above list that are suited to the area you are studying.
2 Name each piece of apparatus chosen.
3 Draw a diagram of each piece.
4 Use each piece of apparatus appropriately.
5 Describe how you used each piece.
6 Record the types of organism collected.

STUDENT REPORT   **Activity**   **2**

Title: _____

_____   *Date:* _____

Apparatus 1

Name of apparatus:
_____
Procedure:
_____
_____
_____
_____
_____
_____
_____

Diagram:

Results:
_____
_____
_____
_____
_____

Name of apparatus:

Procedure:

Diagram:

Results:

Apparatus 3

Name of apparatus:

Procedure:

Diagram:

Results:

Name of apparatus:

Procedure:

Diagram:

Results:

Risks:

_____

_____

_____

_____

Risk management:

_____

_____

_____

_____

Skills:

_____

_____

_____

_____

Skill application:

_____

_____

_____

_____

Conclusions/comments:

_____

_____

_____

_____

Signature:

_____

Activity 3 — To use simple keys to identify any five fauna and any five flora

This type of surveying is referred to as **qualitative** surveying. Using this type of analysis helps us identify the many plants and animals in our habitat. It can be looked at as a health check because the greater the variety of species present, the healthier the habitat. You can use biological plant and animal keys specific to your habitat to identify the different species present. Examples from some of the habitats listed at the beginning of this chapter can be found online at www.edco.ie/lcbiologyexperimentbook. These can be used in conjunction with the keys provided by your teacher. When you have completed your identification, note any adaptations, competitors or interdependence that the species has. From your information, construct a food chain, food web and pyramid of numbers. (Where possible, take all plants and animals back to their original location.)

Materials:

- Hand lens
- Forceps
- Ruler
- Containers
- Identification keys

Procedure:

1 Using the identification keys, identify any five plants and any five animals found in the area of study.
2 Note where each organism was found.
3 Note an adaptation of each organism to the ecosystem.
4 Note their interdependence with other organisms.
5 Note the organisms they compete with.
6 Form a simple food chain from the organisms listed.
7 Form a simple food web using at least nine of these organisms.
8 Draw a pyramid of numbers using some of the organisms listed.
9 Record your results in the tables provided and construct a food chain (four organisms), food web (at least nine organisms) and a pyramid of numbers.

STUDENT REPORT Activity **3**

Title: _____

_____ *Date:* _____

Procedure:

_____

_____

_____

_____

_____

_____

_____

_____

_____

_____

_____

_____

Photographs/diagrams of plants and animals found:

Plants

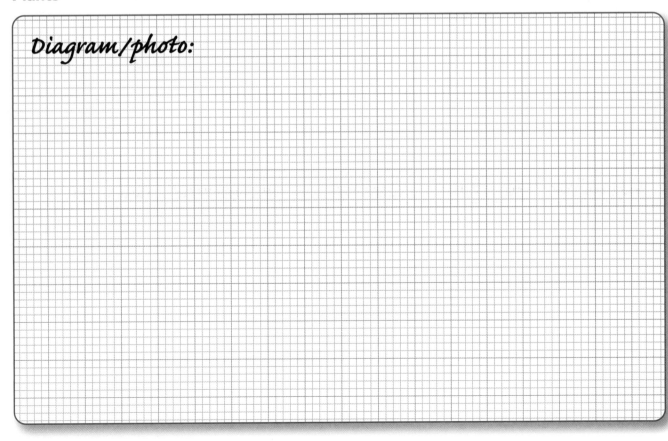

Diagram/photo:

Animals

Diagram/photo:

Results:

Plants identified

Organism name	Where found	Adaptation	Interdependence	Competition

Animals identified

Organism name	Where found	Adaptation	Interdependence	Competition

Food chain:

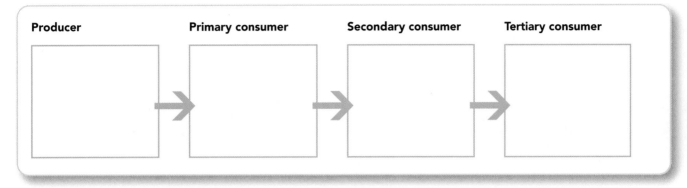

Producer	Primary consumer	Secondary consumer	Tertiary consumer

Food web:

Use the plants and animals from your ecosystem to complete the food web.

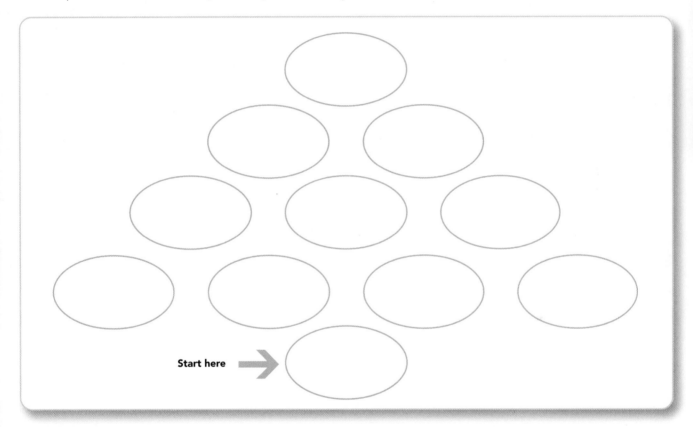

Start here

Pyramid of numbers:

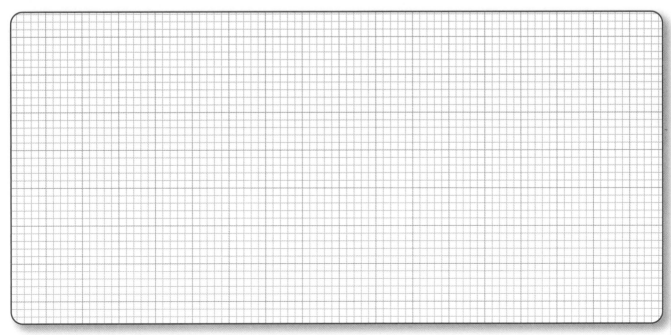

Risks:

Risk management:

Skills:

Skill application:

Conclusions/comments:

Signature:

Activity 4 To carry out a quantitative study of a habitat

A **quantitative study** involves determining the number of a particular species present in the habitat. One or more of the following methods can be used to carry out a quantitative study of a habitat.

- Direct count
- Population density (n/m²)
- Percentage frequency
- Percentage cover
- Capture–recapture
- Belt/line transect

Direct count

Useful in grassland or woodland, for example to estimate the number of large trees.

Procedure:

1 Count the number of large trees (e.g. horse chestnut trees) or large animals (e.g. deer) in the area.
2 Repeat the procedure three times and take the average.

Results:

Direct count

Organism name	Count 1	Count 2	Count 3	Average

Population density – number of species/m²

Materials:

- Frame quadrat
- Pencil

Procedure:

1 Select a sample area and mark it off.
2 Decide on and record the organisms to be studied.
3 Throw a small object over your shoulder to select a random sample point.
4 Place the quadrat at the random sample point.
5 Record the number of the named organisms, e.g. daisies, within the quadrat.
6 Repeat for a total of 10 throws.
7 Calculate the average number per m². (Note: each quadrat has an area of (0.5) x (0.5) m² = 0.25m², so multiply your final answer by 4 to get the average number/m².)
8 Write your results in the table below and then draw a bar chart or histogram to illustrate your data.

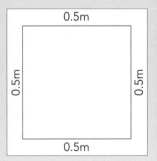

Results:

Population density

Sample calculation:

Population of daisies in a parkland: 320 daisies in 20 quadrats.
Use the formula below to estimate the population density:

$$\text{Population density/m}^2 = \frac{\text{Total number of organisms}}{\text{Total number of quadrats thrown}} \times 4$$

$$\text{Population density of daisies} = \frac{320}{20} \times 4 = 64/\text{m}^2$$

Name of organism	Number of organisms per quadrat										Population density (number of species/m²)
	1	2	3	4	5	6	7	8	9	10	

Histogram/bar chart:

Percentage frequency

Percentage frequency is the chance of finding a named species with any one throw of the quadrat. This is useful in woodland, grassland and bog.

Materials:

- Frame quadrat
- Pencil

Procedure:

1 Select a sample area and mark it off.
2 Decide on and record the organisms to be studied.
3 Throw a small object over your shoulder to select a random sample point.
4 Place the quadrat at the random sample point.
5 Record the presence or absence of the named organisms within the quadrat.
6 Repeat for a total of 10 throws.
7 Calculate percentage frequency using the formula below.
8 Fill in the chart and draw a histogram or bar chart of the results.

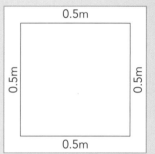

Use this formula to calculate the % frequency of a number of organisms:

$$\% \text{ frequency} = \frac{\text{Number of quadrats containing organism}}{\text{Number of quadrats thrown}} \times 100$$

Sample calculation:
Daisies found in 7 of 10 quadrat throws

$$\% \text{ frequency} = \frac{7}{10} \times 100 = 70\%$$

Results:

Name of organism	Quadrat										% frequency
	1	2	3	4	5	6	7	8	9	10	

Histogram/bar chart:

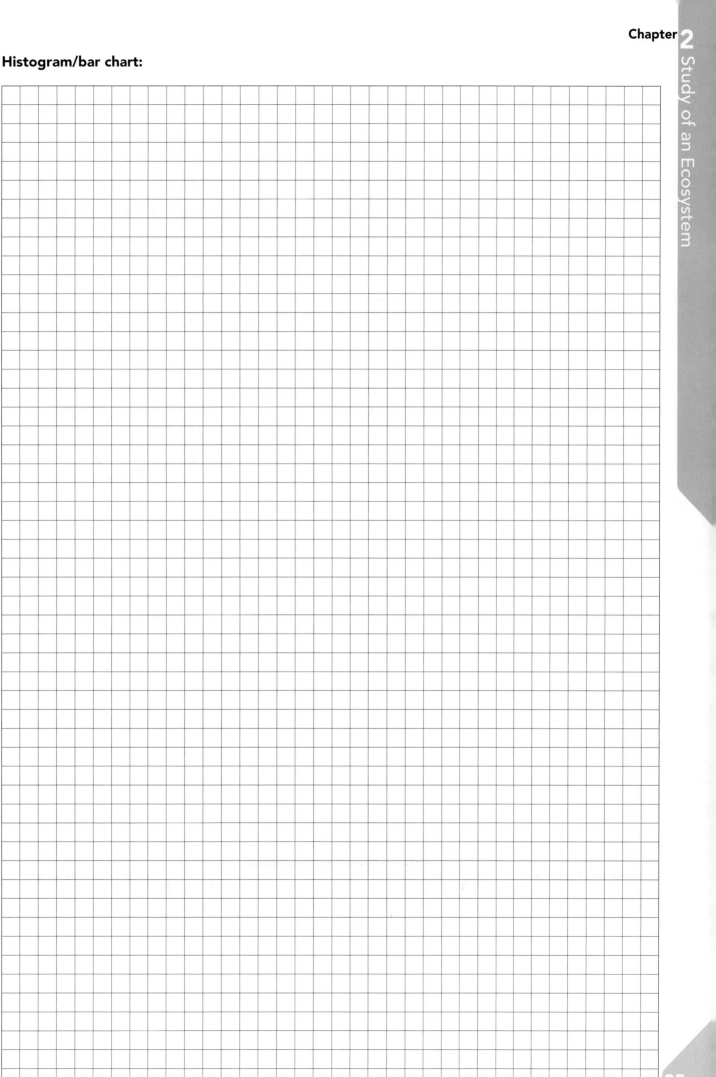

Percentage cover

Percentage cover is an estimate of the amount of ground in a quadrat covered by a named species. It is useful in woodland, grassland, bog and seashore.

Materials:

- Grid quadrat
- Pencil
- Needle

Procedure:

1 Select a sample area and mark it off.
2 Decide on and record the organisms to be studied.
3 Throw a small, light object over your shoulder to select a random sample point.
4 Place the quadrat at the random sample point.
5 Lower the needle at each sampling point on the quadrat and note the presence or absence of the named organism, i.e. the number of times the needle hits the organism being surveyed.
6 Calculate percentage cover using the formula below.
7 Repeat for a total of ten throws.
8 Calculate the average percentage cover.
9 Repeat steps 3–8 for each named organism.
10 Record the data on a bar chart, histogram or pie chart.

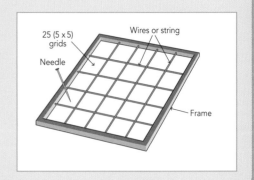

Sample result and calculation for 12 hits recorded with grid quadrat:

Grid quadrat

0.5m

$$\% \ cover \ = \ \frac{Number \ of \ hits}{Number \ of \ grids} \times 100$$

$$\% \ cover \ = \ \frac{12}{25} \times 100 = 48\%$$

Results:

Name of organism	Percentage cover per quadrat										Average % cover
	1	2	3	4	5	6	7	8	9	10	

Histogram/bar chart/pie chart:

Belt transect

Belt transect is a non-random technique used where there are obvious different regions in the same habitat. It is useful in seashore, woodland, bog and grassland.

Materials:

- Tape measure (30m)
- Two tent pegs
- Frame/grid quadrat

Procedure:

1 Select the sample area and stretch the tape across it.
2 Use the tent pegs to secure the tape at each end so that it remains taut.
3 Decide on and record the organisms to be studied.
4 Place the quadrat at the 0m mark on the tape.
5 Note the number, frequency (or calculate % cover) of each named organism in the quadrat.
6 Repeat at suitable intervals along the tape.
7 Record your results in the table provided.
8 Represent your results as a histogram/bar chart.

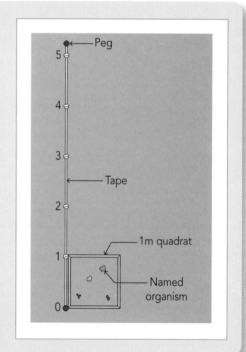

Results:

Named organism	Position of quadrat on belt transect												
	0m												

Histogram/bar chart:

Capture–recapture

This technique is used when there are too many animals for a direct count.

Materials:

■ Suitable markers   ■ Suitable capture apparatus

Procedure:

1 Select the sample area and mark it off.
2 Decide on the animal to be studied (e.g. garden snail).
3 Search the area for the chosen animal.
4 Mark each animal found in a suitable manner. (Make sure the marking material does not contain harmful solvents or is so bright or large that it might expose the animal to a predator.)
5 Count and record the number of animals captured and marked (e.g. 30).
6 Return each animal to where it was found.
7 Return to the area the following day.
8 Search for the animals in the same way.
9 Count and record the number of animals captured the second time (e.g. 30).
10 Count and record the number of marked animals in the second sample – the recaptured sample (e.g. 6).
11 Return each animal to where it was found.
12 Use the formula below to calculate the total number of animals in the sample area.

$$\text{Population} = \frac{\text{Number captured 1st time} \times \text{number captured 2nd time}}{\text{Number recaptured}}$$

Sample result and calculation:

Number captured on first visit = 30
Number captured on second visit = 30
Number recaptured = 6

$$\text{Total population} = \frac{30 \times 30}{6} = 150$$

Results:

Number of animals captured and marked on 1st visit	
Number of animals captured on 2nd visit	
Number of marked animals in recaptured sample	
Total population of animals	

STUDENT REPORT   Activity   **4**

Outline two procedures used.

Procedure 1

Title: _____

_____   *Date:* _____

Procedure:

_____

_____

_____

_____

_____

_____

_____

_____

_____

_____

_____

_____

_____

_____

Diagram (apparatus):

Procedure 2

Title: _____

_____ *Date:* _____

Procedure:

_____

_____

_____

_____

_____

_____

_____

_____

_____

_____

_____

_____

_____

Diagram (apparatus):

Risks:

_____
_____
_____
_____

Risk management:

_____
_____
_____
_____

Skills:

_____
_____
_____
_____
_____

Skill application:

_____
_____
_____
_____
_____

Conclusions/comments:

_____
_____
_____
_____
_____

Signature:

_____

Activity 5 · To investigate three abiotic factors in a selected ecosystem

The following is a list of abiotic factors as outlined in the Leaving Certificate Biology Syllabus.

- pH
- Air temperature
- Ground temperature
- Aquatic temperature
- Light intensity

- Water current
- Air current
- Dissolved oxygen
- Mineral content
- Percentage air in soil

- Percentage water in soil
- Percentage humus
- Salinity
- Degree of exposure
- Slope

Materials:

- Pieces of equipment to measure the chosen abiotic factors

Procedure:

1 Choose any three abiotic factors from the list above.
2 Gather the equipment necessary to measure these abiotic factors.
3 Familiarise yourself with how to use the equipment.
4 Measure the abiotic factors. Take three readings in each case.
5 Link these abiotic factors to plant/animal adaptations.
6 Record the results and how you measured them in the tables below.

STUDENT REPORT Activity 5

Title: _____

_____ Date: _____

Abiotic factor 1

Abiotic factor: _____
Apparatus used: _____
Procedure: _____
_____
_____
_____
_____
_____
_____

Diagram:

Abiotic factor 2

Abiotic factor:

Apparatus used:

Procedure:

Diagram:

Abiotic factor: _____

Apparatus used: _____

Procedure: _____

_____

_____

_____

_____

_____

_____

Diagram:

Results:

Abiotic factor	Apparatus used	Reading 1	Reading 2	Reading 3	Average

Results:

Abiotic factor	Plant/animal	Adaptation

Risks:

_____
_____
_____
_____
_____

Risk management:

_____
_____
_____
_____
_____

Skills:

_____
_____
_____
_____
_____

Skill application:

_____
_____
_____
_____
_____

Conclusions/comments:

_____
_____
_____
_____

Signature:

Activities **2–5** Questions

1 Explain each of the following terms:

Ecology _____

_____

Ecosystem _____

_____

Habitat _____

_____

Producer _____

_____

Consumer _____

_____

2 Distinguish between the terms *flora* and *fauna*.

_____

_____

3 Name five plants found in the ecosystem you have studied.

_____

_____

_____

_____

_____

4 In the space below draw up a simple key which could be used to identify each of these plants.

5 Name five animals found in the ecosystem you have studied.

_____

_____

_____

_____

_____

6 In the space below draw up a simple key which could be used to identify each of these animals.

7 Give two different food chains from the ecosystem you have studied.

_____

_____

8 Draw a pyramid of numbers to represent one of the above food chains.

9 Draw a food web from the ecosystem you have studied.

10 Explain what is meant by *trophic levels* and state how many are indicated in the food web you have given.

_____

_____

_____

_____

_____

11 What factors do plants compete for in their ecosystems?

_____

_____

_____

12 What factors do animals compete for in their ecosystems?

_____

_____

_____

13 Distinguish between intra-specific and inter-specific competition.

_____

_____

_____

14 Explain the following terms:

Predator   _____

_____

Parasite   _____

_____

Symbiosis   _____

_____

15 What is a profile map?

_____

_____

_____

16 What is an identification key?

_____

17 Distinguish between a qualitative study and a quantitative study.

_____

_____

18 What is a quadrat?

_____

19 Is a quadrat more suited for use when carrying out a quantitative study of plants or of animals?

_____

20 If you were to calculate the population density of barnacles on a seashore, briefly describe the method you would use.

_____

_____

_____

21 If you were to calculate the population density of field mice, briefly describe the method you would use.

_____

_____

_____

22 When carrying out a quantitative study, why might a line transect be used instead of a quadrat?

_____

_____

23 Explain the term _abiotic factor_.

_____

_____

24 Name three abiotic factors that influence the ecosystem you have studied.

_____

_____

_____

25 Explain the term _adaptation_.

_____

_____

26 Name an organism identified in the ecosystem you have studied and give an adaptation feature that you noted. Explain how this adaptation feature is of benefit to the organism.

_____

_____

_____

_____

_____

Examination note

These activities were examined in Section B of the Leaving Cert Biology Exam in **2008** (HL), **2007** (OL), **2006** (HL and OL) and **2004** (OL).

They also appeared in Section C in **2011** (HL) Q10c, in **2009** (HL) Q11c, in **2008** (OL) Q10b, in **2007** (OL) Q10c, in **2006** (HL) Q10b and in **2005** (HL) Q12c, (OL) Q10b.

Chapter **3** | The Microscope

Activity 6 To be familiar with and to use a light microscope

Materials:

■ Light microscope   ■ Prepared slides

Procedure:

1 Study the microscope carefully and identify each part.
2 Plug in the microscope and turn on the light source.
3 Rotate the nosepiece so that the low power lens is clicked into position.
4 Put a prepared microscope slide on the stage.
5 Move the slide until the object to be viewed is above the hole in the stage. Use the stage clips to hold the slide in position.
6 Using the coarse focus wheel, bring the objective lens and slide as close together as possible. Watch carefully from the side to make sure the lens does not hit the slide.
7 Looking down the eyepiece, adjust the iris diaphragm to find the most suitable level of illumination.
8 Use the coarse focus wheel to bring the object into focus. If necessary, readjust the iris diaphragm.
9 Rotate the nosepiece so that the medium power lens is clicked into position.
10 Refocus using the coarse focus wheel and fine focus wheel.
11 If necessary, readjust the illumination.
12 Rotate the nosepiece so that the high power lens is clicked into position. Refocus using the fine focus wheel only. Extreme care must be taken at this point as the lens is very close to the slide.
13 Draw labelled diagrams of what you see at low power and at high power.

(Diagram of a light microscope with the following labels: Eyepiece, Arm, Revolving nosepiece, Objective lens, Stage, Iris diaphragm, Coarse focus, Lever, Condenser, Light source, Base, Fine focus)

Note: Total magnification = eyepiece x objective lens.

STUDENT REPORT Activity **6**

Title: _____

_____ *Date:* _____

Procedure:

_____
_____
_____
_____
_____
_____
_____
_____
_____
_____
_____
_____
_____
_____
_____
_____

Results:

Low power x

High power x

Risks:
_____
_____
_____

Risk management:
_____
_____
_____
_____

Skills:
_____
_____
_____

Skill application:
_____
_____
_____
_____

Conclusions/comments:
_____
_____
_____
_____

Signature:
_____

Activity 6 Questions

1 Identify the parts labelled and state the function of each part:

Label	Part	Function
A		
B		
C		
D		
E		
F		

2 If the lenses used on a microscope show x10 and x4, what is the total magnification?

_____

3 Why should a slide not be moved when viewing under high-power magnification?

_____

4 Some samples (e.g. a centipede collected in a field study) are too small for the naked eye but too large when viewed under a microscope. How can these samples be viewed?

_____

_____

5 Name the type of microscope used to see the ultrastructure of a cell.

_____

6 State one function of each of the following cell components:

Ribosome _____

Cell membrane _____

Mitochondrion _____

Cell wall _____

Chloroplast _____

Vacuole _____

Examination note

This activity was examined in Section B of the Leaving Cert Biology Examination in **2006** (HL) and **2004** (OL).

Activity **7a** To prepare and examine plant (onion) cells, unstained and stained, using the light microscope

Materials:

- Microscope
- Microscope slides
- Cover slips
- Mounted needle
- Forceps
- Petri dish
- Onion
- Chopping board
- Sharp knife
- Small paintbrush
- Droppers
- Water
- Iodine stain
- Absorbent paper

Procedure:

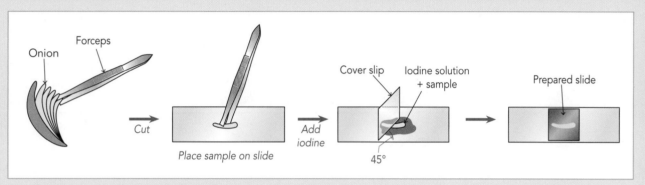

1. Set up microscope.
2. Place a drop of water on a slide.
3. Cut the onion in half and locate some epidermal tissue.
4. Peel off the epidermis with forceps.
5. Cut it into small pieces.
6. Put these pieces into water in a Petri dish.
7. Transfer one piece into the drop of water on the slide using the small paintbrush.
8. Place a cover slip at the edge of the water at an angle of 45° to the slide.
9. Slowly lower the cover slip onto the water, supporting it with a mounted needle to avoid trapping air bubbles.
10. Dry the slide with absorbent paper.
11. Examine under the microscope.
12. Repeat the above steps using iodine stain instead of water.
13. Draw labelled diagrams at low power (x40) and at high power (x400).

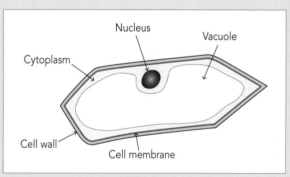

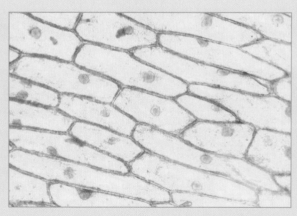

STUDENT REPORT Activity **7a**

Title: _____

_____ *Date:* _____

Procedure:

_____
_____
_____
_____
_____
_____
_____
_____
_____
_____
_____
_____
_____
_____
_____
_____

Results:

Low power x

High power x

Risks: _____
_____
_____

Risk management: _____
_____
_____
_____

Skills: _____
_____
_____

Skill application: _____
_____
_____
_____

Conclusions/comments: _____
_____
_____

Signature: _____

Activity 7a Questions

1 The onion can be described as a modified leaf. For what purpose is it modified?

_____

2 The onion can also be described as a perennating organ. Explain what *perennating* means.

_____

3 Define *organ*. _____

_____

4 Why is the removed epidermal tissue placed in water?

_____

_____

5 Describe the correct method of placing the epidermal tissue on the slide.

_____

_____

6 Describe the correct method of placing the cover slip on the sample.

_____

_____

7 In what order should the objective lenses be used to view the sample?

_____

_____

8 Why should the objective lenses be used in this order?

_____

_____

9 What stain is used in this activity?

_____

10 If excess liquid is seen on the slide, how should it be removed?

_____

_____

11 State two features of onion cells that indicate that they are typical plant cells.

_____

_____

12 In the space below, draw and label onion cells as viewed under high power magnification.

Examination note

This activity was examined in Section B of the Leaving Cert Biology Exam in **2011** (OL), **2010** (HL) and **2004** (OL).

Activity 7b To prepare and examine animal (cheek) cells, unstained and stained, using the light microscope

Materials:

- Microscope
- Microscope slides
- Cover slips

- Cotton buds
- Mounted needle
- Droppers

- Water
- Methylene blue stain (1%)
- Absorbent paper

Procedure:

1 Set up microscope.
2 Swab inside cheek surface with a cotton bud (or with a clean finger).
3 Transfer the cells to the slide.
4 Cover with one drop of water.
5 Place a cover slip at the edge of the water at an angle of 45° to the slide.
6 Slowly lower the cover slip onto the water, supporting it with a mounted needle to avoid trapping air bubbles.
7 Dry the slide with absorbent paper.
8 Examine under the microscope.
9 Repeat the above steps using methylene blue stain instead of water.
10 Draw labelled diagrams at low power (x40) and at high power (x400).

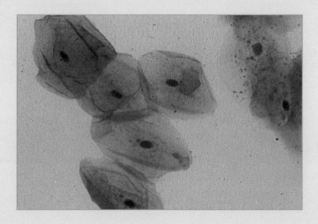

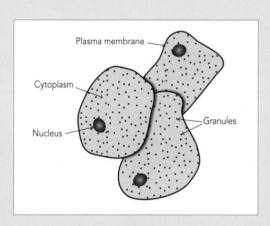

STUDENT REPORT   Activity   **7b**

Title: _____

_____ *Date:* _____

Procedure:
_____
_____
_____
_____
_____
_____
_____
_____
_____
_____
_____
_____
_____
_____
_____

Results:

Low power x

High power x

Risks:

Risk management:

Skills:

Skill application:

Conclusions/comments:

Signature:

Activity 7b Questions

1 State two differences between plant cells and animal cells.

_____

_____

2 Describe how the cheek cells are obtained and transferred to the microscope slide.

_____

_____

3 What stain is used in this activity? _____

4 Why is a stain used? _____

_____

5 How is the stain applied? _____

_____

6 If excess liquid is seen on the slide, how should it be removed?

_____

_____

7 Why is a cover slip used? _____

_____

8 Why is the cover slip lowered from an angle of 45° onto the slide?

_____

_____

9 Why is the sample viewed under low power magnification first?

_____

10 What type of tissue is found on the inside of the human cheek?

_____

11 Define _tissue_.

_____

_____

12 In the space below, draw and label human cheek cells as viewed under high power magnification.

```
┌──────────────────────────────────────────────────────────────┐
│                                                                │
│                                                                │
│                                                                │
│                                                                │
│                                                                │
│                                                                │
│                                                                │
│                                                                │
│                                                                │
│                                                                │
└──────────────────────────────────────────────────────────────┘
```

Examination note

This activity was examined in Section B of the Leaving Cert Biology Exam in **2010** (HL) and **2006** (HL).

Chapter **4** Enzymes

Activity **8** To investigate the effect of pH on the rate of catalase activity

Theory:

An **enzyme** is a **biological catalyst**. Catalysts are chemicals that speed up chemical reactions without being altered themselves. All enzymes are proteins, which are large molecules. In its activity as catalyst, a section of the enzyme fits ideally with the substrate (the material that undergoes reaction). These three-dimensional active sites are sensitive to changes in their environment that differ from ideal conditions. These ideal conditions, where an enzyme works at its most efficient level, are referred to as **optimum conditions**.

In the following activities you will investigate the effect of changing temperature and pH on enzyme activity. You will also investigate the effect of heat denaturation on enzyme activity. When the temperature is raised above 60°C, the active sites change completely in shape and no longer fit with the substrate. This change is irreversible and the enzyme is said to be denatured.

The *enzyme* used in these experiments is **catalase** (peroxidase), which is extracted from celery. (A large volume of celery extract is used as only a small percentage of it is catalase.) The *substrate* is **hydrogen peroxide**, which breaks down to release oxygen. The *product* – **oxygen** – is trapped by washing-up liquid, forming a foam. The volume of foam produced in a given time is taken as a measure of enzyme activity.

Materials:

- Catalase source (celery/radish/potato/liver) – fresh samples
- Blender
- Distilled water
- Coffee filter paper/coarse filter paper
- Hydrogen peroxide (20%)
- pH buffers (pH 4, 7, 10, 13)
- Washing-up liquid
- Dropper
- 10cm³ pipette
- 100cm³ graduated cylinder
- Knife
- Chopping board
- Stopwatch
- Water bath
- Thermometer

 Hydrogen peroxide is a corrosive solution; students should use safety glasses and avoid contact with skin.

Procedure:

1. Blend three stalks of celery using a hand blender and add 100cm³ of distilled water.
2. Filter this solution into a 250cm³ beaker using coffee filter paper.
3. Place this solution in a water bath at 25°C.
4. Place 10cm³ of this catalase solution into a 100cm³ graduated cylinder and place in the water bath.

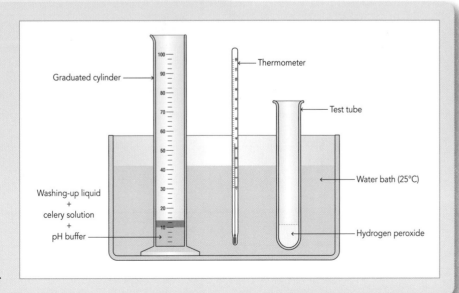

Graduated cylinder

Thermometer

Test tube

Water bath (25°C)

Washing-up liquid
+
celery solution
+
pH buffer

Hydrogen peroxide

Procedure:

5 Add 10cm³ of pH 4 buffer solution to the graduated cylinder.
6 Using a dropper, add one drop of washing-up liquid.
7 Add 5cm³ of hydrogen peroxide into a test tube and place in the water bath.
8 Leave both solutions until they have reached 25°C.
9 Add the hydrogen peroxide to the cylinder.
10 Swirl the cylinder carefully.
11 Start the stopwatch.
12 Note the volume of foam produced after 2 minutes.
13 Repeat using buffers 7, 10 and 13.
14 Draw a graph of the results showing volume of foam against pH.

Note: The pH of the solution can be checked using (a) universal indicator solution or paper (compare the colour change with the chart provided) or (b) a pH metre at any point during this experiment.

STUDENT REPORT   Activity   **8**

Title: _____

_____   Date: _____

Procedure:

_____

_____

_____

_____

_____

_____

_____

_____

_____

_____

_____

_____

_____

_____

_____

_____

_____

_____

_____

Procedure:

_____

_____

_____

_____

_____

_____

_____

_____

_____

_____

_____

_____

_____

_____

_____

_____

_____

_____

Results:

pH buffer	Initial volume (cm^3)	Final volume (cm^3)	Volume of foam (cm^3)
4			
7			
10			
13			

Diagram:

Graph:

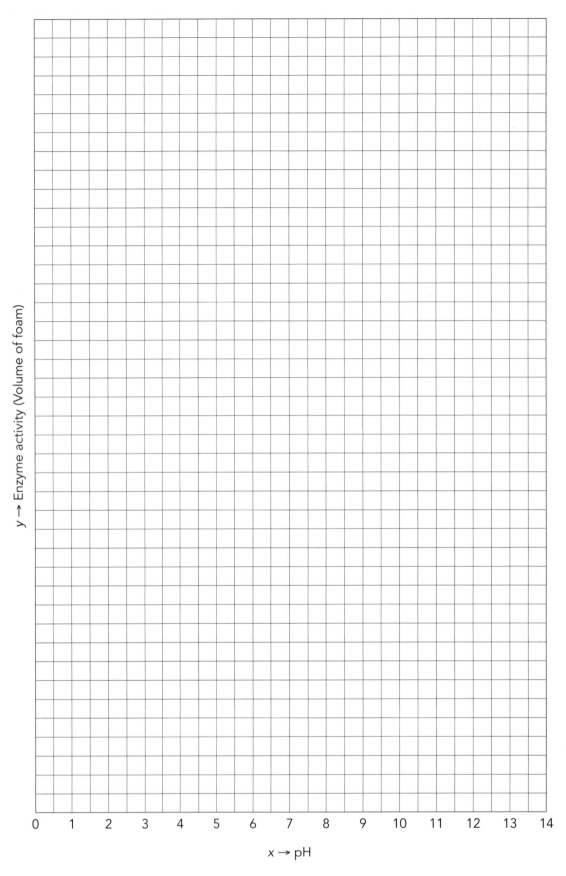

Risks:

_____

_____

_____

_____

Risk management:

_____

_____

_____

_____

Skills:

_____

_____

_____

_____

Skill application:

_____

_____

_____

_____

Conclusions/comments:

_____

_____

_____

_____

Signature:

_____

Activity 8 Questions

1 What is an enzyme? _____

_____

2 Where in a cell are enzymes produced? _____

3 Catalase (peroxidase) is used in this activity. What does the -ase tell you about the chemical?

_____

_____

4 Enzymes are effective in small amounts. Why is such a large volume of celery extract required?

_____

_____

5 Name the substrate in this activity. _____

6 Why are a few drops of washing-up liquid used? _____

_____

7 What are buffer solutions? _____

8 Name one factor that is kept constant during this activity.

_____

9 Describe how this factor is kept constant.

_____

10 How is the rate of activity of the enzyme measured?

_____

11 Graph the results you would expect to find in this activity.

12 What is meant by the term *optimum pH*? _____

_____

_____

13 From your results, what is the optimum pH for catalase activity? _____

Examination note

This activity appears in the **2003** Sample Paper (HL) and was examined in the Leaving Cert Biology exam in **2010** (OL).

Activity 9 — To investigate the effect of temperature on the rate of catalase activity (i.e. the rate of enzyme activity)

Materials:

- Catalase source (celery/radish/potato/liver)
- Blender
- Distilled water
- Coffee filter paper/coarse filter paper
- Hydrogen peroxide (20%)
- pH buffer 9
- Washing-up liquid
- Dropper
- 10cm³ pipette
- 100cm³ graduated cylinder
- Knife
- Chopping board
- Stopwatch
- Water baths 0–60°C
- Thermometers
- Ice

Procedure:

1 Blend three stalks of celery using a hand blender and add 100cm³ of distilled water.

2 Filter this solution into a 250cm³ beaker using coffee filter paper.

3 Place 10cm³ of this catalase solution into a 100cm³ graduated cylinder and place in the ice bath at 0°C.

4 Add 10cm³ of pH 9 buffer solution to the graduated cylinder.

5 Using a dropper, add one drop of washing-up liquid.

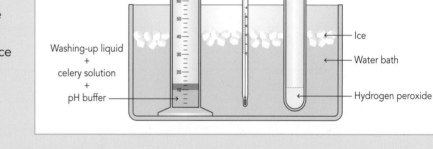

6 Add 5cm³ of hydrogen peroxide into a test tube and place in the ice bath.

7 Leave both solutions until they have reached 0°C.

8 Add the hydrogen peroxide to the cylinder.

9 Swirl the cylinder carefully.

10 Start the stopwatch.

11 Note the volume of foam produced after 2 minutes.

12 Repeat the above steps at four other temperatures, including a sample in the 50–60°C range.

13 Draw a graph of the results showing volume of foam against temperature.

 Hydrogen peroxide is a corrosive solution; students should use safety glasses and avoid contact with skin.

STUDENT REPORT   Activity   9

Title: _____

_____   *Date:* _____

Procedure:

_____
_____
_____
_____
_____
_____
_____
_____
_____
_____
_____
_____
_____
_____
_____
_____
_____
_____
_____
_____
_____
_____
_____
_____
_____
_____
_____

Results:

Temperature (°C)	Initial volume (cm³)	Final volume (cm³)	Volume of foam (cm³)
0			
10			
20			
30			
40			
50			
60			

Graph:

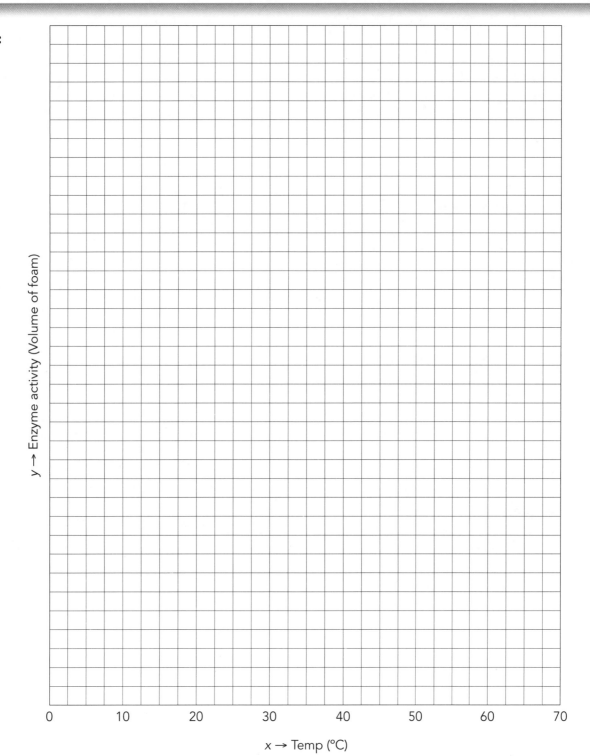

$y \rightarrow$ Enzyme activity (Volume of foam)

$x \rightarrow$ Temp (°C)

Risks:

_____
_____
_____
_____

Risk management:

_____
_____
_____

Skills:

_____
_____
_____
_____

Skill application:

_____
_____
_____

Conclusions/comments:

_____
_____
_____
_____

Signature:

_____

Activity 9 Questions

1 To what group of biomolecules do enzymes belong?

_____

2 Name two enzymes found in the human digestive system and state where they are found.

(i) _____

(ii) _____

3 State the substrates on which the above-named enzymes act.

_____

4 Explain the term *substrate* in relation to enzyme activity.

_____

_____

5 Explain the term *product* in relation to enzyme activity.

_____

_____

6 Name the enzyme in this activity.

_____

7 Name the substrate in this activity.

_____

8 Name the products in this activity.

_____

9 How is the rate of activity of the enzyme measured?

_____

10 Which product causes the foam to rise in the graduated cylinder?

_____

11 Why is the height of the foam taken after 2 minutes at each temperature?

_____

12 How is the temperature varied during the activity?

_____

13 What factor is kept constant during the activity?

_____

14 Describe how this factor is kept constant.

_____

15 Why is the rate of activity not recorded after 60°C?

_____

16 What is meant by a denatured enzyme?

_____

Examination note

This activity was examined in Section B of the Leaving Cert Biology Exam in **2012** (HL and OL), **2007** (HL and OL) and **2005** (OL).

Activity 10 — To (a) prepare an enzyme immobilisation and (b) examine its application

Theory:

An immobilised enzyme is one which is attached to an insoluble surface or covered in a gel. These enzymes are more efficient because they can be reused, are easy to separate and are more economical. Therefore they are widely used in industry, e.g. pharmaceuticals and brewing. This technique ensures the stability of the enzyme because its ability to change shape is reduced when trapped in gel.

Note: All glassware and equipment must be sterilised before use.

Materials:

- Dried yeast
- Filter funnel
- Sodium alginate
- Filter paper
- Calcium chloride
- Sucrose solution
- Distilled water
- Glucose test strips
- Beakers
- Timer
- 10cm³ syringe
- Suitable filter, e.g. drinking straw

Procedure:

(a) Preparation of immobilised enzyme

1 Add 0.4g of sodium alginate to 10cm³ of distilled water in a 100cm³ beaker.
2 Add 2g of yeast to 10cm³ of distilled water in a separate 100cm³ beaker.
3 Add 1.5g of calcium chloride to 100cm³ of distilled water in a 250cm³ beaker.
4 Thoroughly mix the yeast and sodium alginate solutions.
5 Place 10cm³ of this mixture in a syringe.
6 Slowly, 1cm³ at a time, add this solution to the calcium chloride solution.
7 Beads of the immobilised yeast which contain enzyme will form in the calcium alginate gel.
8 Allow these beads to harden for 15 minutes.
9 Filter the beads and rinse with distilled water. This removes any excess yeast cells which may be attached to the outside of the beads.
10 The beads may be allowed to dry or stored in distilled water.

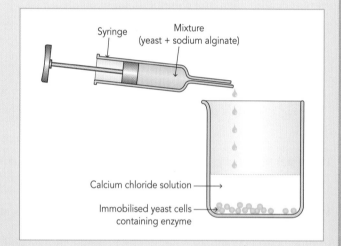

Syringe — Mixture (yeast + sodium alginate)
Calcium chloride solution
Immobilised yeast cells containing enzyme

Procedure:

(b) Application of immobilised enzyme

1 Prepare a free yeast solution as above (2g of dried yeast in 10cm³ distilled water).
2 Pour this solution into a separating funnel and label.
3 Pour the beads of the immobilised enzyme into another funnel and label.
4 Place a suitable filter (e.g. drinking straw) in this funnel to prevent the beads clogging the exit hole.
5 Place 50cm³ of the prepared sucrose solution into each of the separating funnels.
6 Open the taps of the separating funnels and release the enzyme solutions into separate beakers.
7 Using glucose testing strips (Clinistix), test both solutions immediately for the presence of glucose.
8 Note the cloudiness of the solution.
9 Repeat every 30 seconds recording results until glucose is detected.

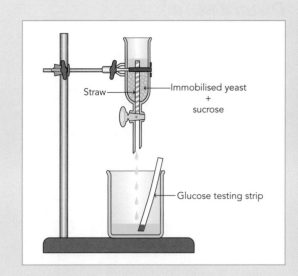

STUDENT REPORT | **Activity** 10

Title: _____

_____ *Date:* _____

Procedure (a): Preparation of enzyme immobilisation

Diagram (a):

Procedure (b): Application of immobilised enzyme

Diagram (b):

Results:

Time (seconds)	Presence of glucose in free yeast solution	Cloudiness of free yeast solution	Presence of glucose in immobilised enzyme solution	Cloudiness of immobilised enzyme solution
0				
30				
60				
90				
120				
150				
180				
210				
240				

Risks:

_____
_____
_____
_____

Risk management:

_____
_____
_____
_____

Skills:

_____
_____
_____
_____

Skill application:

_____
_____
_____
_____

Conclusions/comments:

_____
_____
_____
_____

Signature:

_____

Activity 10 Questions

1 To which kingdom do yeasts belong? _____

2 What is an immobilised enzyme?

_____

3 Name the enzyme/cell that is immobilised in this activity.

_____

4 What is a bioreactor? _____

5 Why is all glassware sterilised prior to carrying out this activity?

_____

6 Why is distilled water used in this activity?

_____

7 What is the purpose of the sodium alginate?

_____

8 Why is such a small quantity of water used to form the yeast and sodium alginate mixture?

_____

9 What is the purpose of the calcium chloride?

_____

10 Why is a syringe used to transfer the yeast/sodium alginate mixture to the calcium chloride solution?

_____

11 Why are the beads left for 15 minutes in the calcium chloride solution?

_____

12 Why are the beads washed with distilled water?

_____

13 When examining the application of the immobilised enzyme:

(i) Why is sucrose used? _____

_____

(ii) Why are glucose testing strips used? _____

_____

14 What is the difference in appearance between the free yeast solution and the immobilised yeast solution?

_____

15 It was noted during testing that glucose was slow to appear in the immobilised yeast solution. Comment on this.

_____

_____

Examination note

This activity was examined in Section B of the Leaving Cert Biology Exam in **2009** (HL) and **2005** (HL). It also appeared in Section C **2009** (OL) Q15(c) and **2007** (HL) Q11c.

Activity 11 To investigate the effect of heat denaturation on catalase activity

Theory:

An enzyme is a biological catalyst. **Catalysts** are chemicals that speed up chemical reactions without being altered themselves. All enzymes are proteins, which are large biomolecules. In its activity as catalyst, a section of the enzyme fits ideally with the substrate (the material that undergoes reaction). These three-dimensional active sites are sensitive to changes in their environment that differ from ideal conditions. These ideal conditions are referred to as **optimum conditions**. When the temperature is raised above 60°C, the active sites change completely in shape and no longer fit with the substrate. This change is irreversible and the enzyme is said to be **denatured**.

Materials:

- Catalase source (celery/radish/potato/liver)
- Blender
- Distilled water
- Coarse filter paper/ coffee filter paper
- Hydrogen peroxide (20%)
- pH buffer 9
- Washing-up liquid
- Dropper
- 10cm³ pipette
- 100cm³ graduated cylinder
- Knife
- Chopping board
- Stopwatch
- Water bath
- Thermometer

 Hydrogen peroxide is a corrosive solution; students should use safety glasses and avoid contact with skin.

Procedure:

1 Blend three stalks of celery using a hand blender and add 100cm³ of distilled water.
2 Filter this solution into a 250cm³ beaker using coffee filter paper.
3 Pour half of this solution into another beaker and boil for 10 minutes.
4 Place 10cm³ of this boiled catalase solution into a 100cm³ graduated cylinder and place in the water bath at 25°C.
5 Add 10cm³ of pH 9 buffer solution to the graduated cylinder.
6 Using a dropper, add one drop of washing-up liquid.
7 Add 5cm³ of hydrogen peroxide into a test tube and place in the water bath.
8 Leave both solutions until they have reached 25°C.
9 Add the hydrogen peroxide to the cylinder.
10 Swirl the cylinder carefully.
11 Start the stopwatch.
12 Note the volume of foam produced after 2 minutes.
13 Repeat steps 4–12 using the unboiled catalase solution.

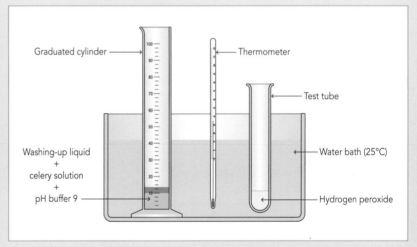

STUDENT REPORT Activity 11

Title: _____

_____ Date: _____

Procedure:

_____
_____
_____
_____
_____
_____
_____
_____
_____
_____
_____
_____
_____
_____
_____
_____
_____
_____
_____
_____
_____
_____
_____
_____
_____
_____

Results:

	Initial volume of foam (cm³)	Final volume of foam (cm³)	Volume of foam (cm³)
Catalase solution Boiled (denatured)			
Catalase solution Unboiled			

Diagram:

Risks:

_____

_____

_____

_____

Risk management:

_____

_____

_____

Skills:

_____

_____

_____

Skill application:

_____

_____

_____

Conclusions/comments:

_____

_____

_____

Signature: _____

Activity 11 Questions

1 What is an enzyme?

_____

2 To what group of biomolecules do enzymes belong?

_____

3 What is meant by the active site of an enzyme?

_____

4 What is a denatured enzyme?

_____

5 How is the enzyme denatured in this activity?

_____

_____

6 Name two other factors that can cause enzyme denaturation.

_____

_____

7 Name the enzyme used in this activity.

_____

8 Name the substrate used in this activity.

_____

9 What control is used in this activity?

_____

10 How is enzyme activity measured?

_____

11 Name two enzymes in the human digestive system and state where they are found.

_____

12 Name the substrates on which the above named enzymes act.

_____

13 What is the optimum temperature for digestive enzyme activity? Give a reason for your answer.

_____

_____

14 Boiling is used widely as a means of sterilising. Referring to this activity, explain why.

_____

_____

_____

Examination note

This activity was examined in Section B of the Leaving Cert Biology Exam in **2008** (HL).

Chapter **5** | Photosynthesis

To investigate the effect of CO_2 concentration on the rate of photosynthesis

Theory:

The rate of photosynthesis is controlled by three main factors. These are known as **limiting factors** (i.e. by changing their concentrations we alter the rate of photosynthesis). The factors are: light intensity; temperature; and CO_2 concentration. During this experiment, the temperature is kept constant by placing the apparatus in a water bath at 25°C, and light intensity is kept constant by placing a lamp a constant distance from the apparatus. The plant used is Canadian pondweed (*Elodea*) and the rate of photosynthesis is measured by counting the number of bubbles of O_2 released every minute. The oxygen produced is stored in air spaces in the stem. This oxygen is forced out of the stem by pressure. The greater the rate of photosynthesis, the more O_2 is produced.

■ The plant used must be well illuminated prior to the experiment.
■ Use fresh stem samples for the best results.

Materials:

■ Pondweed
■ Bench lamp
■ Sodium hydrogen carbonate solutions (0.02%–0.1%)
■ Stopwatch
■ Thermometer
■ Test tube
■ Water bath at 25°C

Procedure:

1 Cut the stem of a piece of pondweed at an angle.
2 Place the pondweed in the test tube, cut end upwards.
3 Add 0.02% sodium hydrogen carbonate solution to the test tube.
4 Place the test tube in a water bath at 25°C.
5 Place the bench lamp 15cm from the apparatus and switch it on.
6 Allow this system to stabilise over 5 minutes.
7 Count the number of O_2 bubbles produced in 1 minute.
8 Repeat three times and find the average.
9 Repeat this procedure using 0.04%, 0.06%, 0.08% and 0.1% solutions.
10 Record your results and draw a graph of oxygen production against sodium hydrogen carbonate concentration.

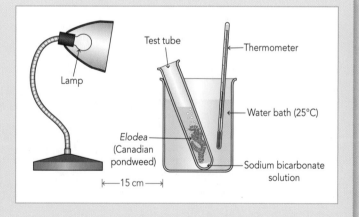

STUDENT REPORT Activity **12a**

Title: _____

_____ *Date:* _____

Procedure:

_____
_____
_____
_____
_____
_____
_____
_____
_____
_____
_____
_____
_____
_____
_____
_____
_____
_____
_____
_____
_____
_____
_____
_____
_____

Results:

Sodium hydrogen carbonate (NaHCO₂)	Reading 1	Reading 2	Reading 3	Average number of bubbles per minute
0.02%				
0.04%				
0.06%				
0.08%				
0.1%				

Graph:

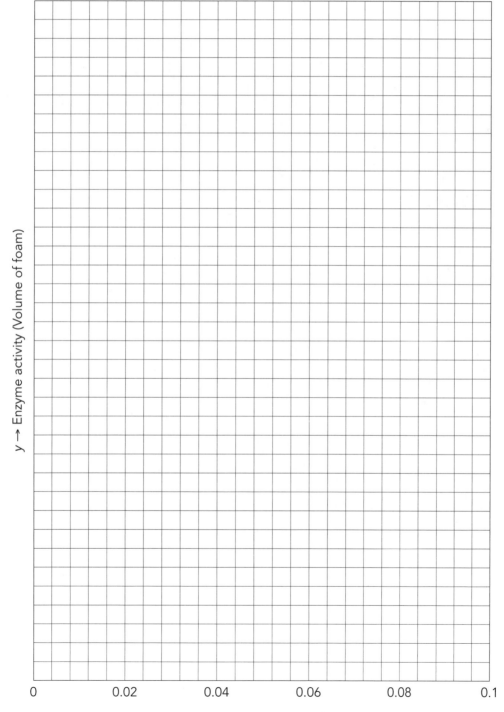

$y \rightarrow$ Enzyme activity (Volume of foam)

$x \rightarrow$ Concentration CO_2 (% CO_2)

0   0.02   0.04   0.06   0.08   0.1

Risks:

_____
_____
_____
_____

Risk management:

_____
_____
_____

Skills:

_____
_____
_____

Skill application:

_____
_____
_____

Conclusions/comments:

_____
_____
_____

Signature:

Activity 12b To investigate the effect of light intensity on the rate of photosynthesis

Theory:

The rate of photosynthesis is controlled by three main factors. These are known as **limiting factors** (i.e. by changing their concentrations we alter the rate of photosynthesis). The factors are: light intensity, temperature and CO_2 concentration. During this experiment, the temperature is kept constant by placing the apparatus in a water bath at 25°C and CO_2 concentration is kept constant by using a 0.1% (1g/litre) of sodium hydrogen carbonate solution. The plant used is Canadian pondweed (*Elodea*) because the bubbles are easy to see. The rate of photosynthesis is measured by counting the number of bubbles of O_2 released every minute. It is important to note that the pondweed should be kept below water to allow you to see the bubbles being released. If the bubbles stop, the stem can be rubbed gently to aid release of oxygen or it can be recut and the experiment continued. If, on the other hand, the rate of flow is too fast to count, for low concentrations the stem can be pinched with a forceps to slow down the rate.

- The plant used must be well illuminated prior to the experiment.
- Use fresh stem samples for the best results.

Materials:

- Pondweed
- Bench lamp
- Sodium hydrogen carbonate solution (0.1%)
- Stopwatch
- Thermometer
- Test tube
- Water bath
- Metre stick

Procedure:

1 Cut the stem of a piece of pond weed at an angle.
2 Place the pondweed in the test tube, cut end upwards.
3 Add 0.1% sodium hydrogen carbonate (10g/litre of distilled water) solution to the test tube.
4 Place the test tube in a water bath at 25°C.
5 Place the bench lamp 1m from the apparatus and switch it on.
6 Allow this system to stabilise over 5 minutes.
7 Count the number of O_2 bubbles produced in 1 minute.
8 Repeat three times and find the average.
9 Repeat this procedure with the plant at 80cm, 60cm, 40cm and 20cm from the lamp.
10 Record your results and draw a graph of oxygen bubbles per minute against $10\,000/d^2$ where d is the distance of the lamp from the beaker in centimetres.

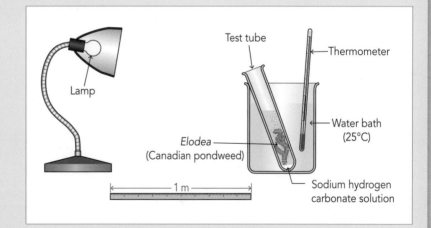

STUDENT REPORT   Activity   **12b**

Title: _____

_____ *Date:* _____

Procedure:

Results:

Distance (cm)	$\dfrac{10\,000}{d^2}$ (cm²) (x-axis)	Reading 1	Reading 2	Reading 3	Average number of bubbles per minute
100	1.00				
80	1.56				
60	2.78				
40	6.25				
20	25.00				

Graph:

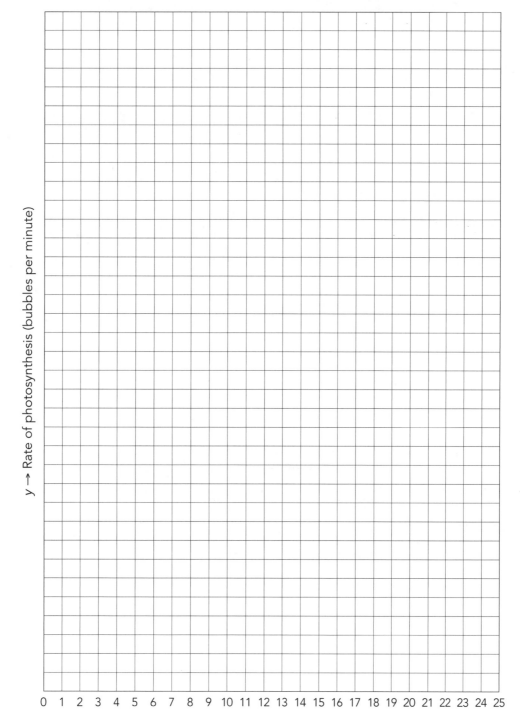

$y \rightarrow$ Rate of photosynthesis (bubbles per minute)

0 1 2 3 4 5 6 7 8 9 10 11 12 13 14 15 16 17 18 19 20 21 22 23 24 25

$$x \rightarrow \text{Distance} \quad \frac{10\,000}{d^2}\ (\text{cm}^2)$$

Risks:

_____
_____
_____
_____

Risk management:

_____
_____
_____
_____

Skills:

_____
_____
_____
_____

Skill application:

_____
_____
_____
_____

Conclusions/comments:

_____
_____
_____
_____

Signature:

_____

Activity 12 Questions

1 What is photosynthesis?

_____

_____

2 Write a balanced equation for photosynthesis.

_____

3 Name the cell organelle where photosynthesis occurs.

_____

4 Name three environmental factors that influence the rate of photosynthesis.

(i) _____

(ii) _____

(iii) _____

5 State the precise role of each of the following in photosynthesis:

Carbon dioxide _____

_____

Water _____

_____

6 Name the plant used in this activity.

_____

7 Why is an aquatic plant used in this activity?

_____

8 When investigating the effect of CO_2 concentration or light intensity on the rate of photosynthesis, certain conditions are kept constant while others are varied. Complete the following chart to show these conditions.

	Name of condition	How achieved
Condition kept constant		
Condition varied – 1		
Condition varied – 2		

9 What is meant by light saturation?

_____

_____

10 How is the rate of photosynthesis measured?

_____

11 What are limiting factors?

_____

_____

12 From your practical activities, name three limiting factors in photosynthesis.

(i) _____

(ii) _____

(iii) _____

13 If this activity were carried out in green light, what result would you expect?

_____

_____

14 Give a reason for your answer in question 13.

_____

_____

Examination note

This activity was examined in Section B of the Leaving Cert Biology Exam in **2010** (HL) and **2007** (HL).
It also appeared in Section C in **2011** (HL) Q14a, (OL) Q12b; **2010** (OL) Q12c; **2009** (HL) Q12c; **2008** (OL) Q12c; and **2004** (HL) Q11c, (OL) Q13c.

Chapter **6** | Fermentation

Activity 13 To prepare and show the production of alcohol by yeast

Theory:

Respiration is the controlled release of energy in a cell, which is brought about by the activity of enzymes on carbohydrates. There are two main types of respiration.

1 Aerobic respiration involves the presence of oxygen.

2 Anaerobic respiration is when no oxygen is involved in the biochemical process.

In this experiment, we investigate the activities of the enzymes in yeast on glucose. The anaerobic conditions are achieved by using oil or a fermentation lock. The alcohol produced in this experiment is **ethanol**. The presence of ethanol is confirmed by carrying out the iodoform test.

Note: All glassware and equipment must be sterilised before use.

Part 1: Production of alcohol

Method 1 Using boiled glucose solution and an oil layer

Materials:

- Dried yeast (or immobilised yeast cells)
- Glucose solution (5%)
- Two 500cm³ conical flasks
- Oil
- Boiled water
- Beakers
- Stoppers
- Delivery tubing
- Limewater

Procedure:

1 Add 250cm³ of prepared glucose solution to each conical flask.

2 Add a sachet of dried yeast to one of the flasks and cover the surface with a layer of oil.

3 Attach a stopper and delivery tubing.

4 Place in a water bath at 25°C.

5 Attach a stopper and delivery tubing to the second flask without the yeast and label it 'control'.

6 Place this apparatus in a water bath at 25°C.

7 Place the tubing from both flasks into beakers containing 100cm³ of limewater.

8 Leave both flasks at 25°C for 1 hour or until production of CO_2 bubbles stops.

9 Record your observations (i.e. smell and appearance of solutions).

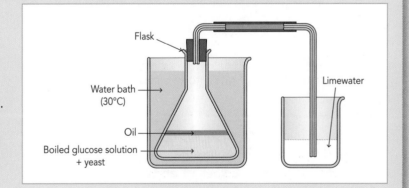

Flask

Water bath (30°C)

Limewater

Oil

Boiled glucose solution + yeast

Method 2 Using a fermentation lock

Materials:

- Dried yeast (or immobilised yeast cells)
- Glucose solution (5%)
- Two 500cm³ conical flasks
- Beakers
- Two fermentation locks

Procedure:

1. Add 250cm³ of prepared glucose solution to each conical flask.
2. Add a sachet of dried yeast to one of the flasks and attach a fermentation lock. The fermentation lock allows gases to exit but none can enter.
3. Attach a fermentation lock to the second flask without the yeast and label it 'control'.
4. Half fill each fermentation lock with water.
5. Leave both flasks at 25°C for 1 hour or until production of CO_2 bubbles stops.
6. Record your observations (i.e. smell and appearance of solutions).

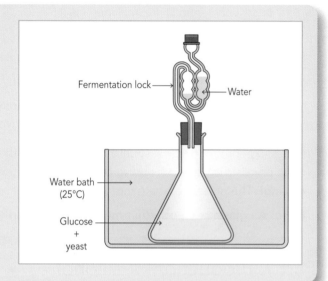

Fermentation lock — Water

Water bath (25°C)

Glucose + yeast

Part 2: Chemical test for alcohol (iodoform test)

Materials:

- Sodium hypochlorite solution (0.5M)
- Potassium iodide solution (0.5M)
- Test tubes
- Droppers
- Hot water bath

 Sodium hypochlorite is a corrosive substance; students should use safety glasses and avoid contact with skin.

Procedure:

1. Filter both yeast solutions.
2. Place 3cm³ of each filtrate into two separate test tubes.
3. To each test tube add 3cm³ of potassium iodide solution and 5cm³ of sodium hypochlorite solution. At first the brown/orange iodine colour will appear.
4. Place both test tubes in a hot water bath and watch for the appearance of pale yellow crystals.
5. Record your results.

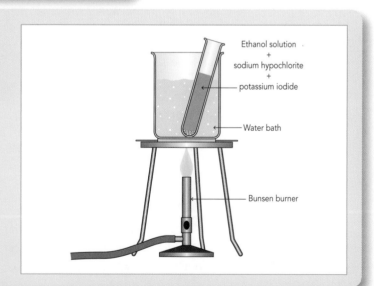

Ethanol solution + sodium hypochlorite + potassium iodide

Water bath

Bunsen burner

Alternative test: In the breathalyser test, acidified sodium dichromate goes from orange to green in the presence of alcohol when placed in a water bath at 80°C. (EU regulations state that students may not perform this test.)

STUDENT REPORT | Activity **13**

Title: _____

_____ *Date:* _____

Procedure:

_____
_____
_____
_____
_____
_____
_____
_____
_____
_____
_____
_____
_____
_____
_____
_____

Results:

Part 1: Production of alcohol

Method 1
_____

_____

Method 2
_____

_____

Part 2: Chemical test for alcohol

Method 1
_____

_____

Method 2
_____

_____

Diagram:

Risks:

Risk management:

Skills:

Skill application:

Conclusions/comments:

Signature:

Activity 13 Questions

1 Define respiration.

2 Distinguish between aerobic and anaerobic respiration.

3 What is fermentation?

4 Is fermentation affected by temperature? Explain your answer.

5 Why must all glassware be sterilised before the activity?

6 Describe how the glassware is sterilised.

7 Name the substance (substrate) that yeast feeds on during this activity.

8 Name the two products of the reaction.

(i)

(ii)

9 What control is used in this activity?

10 How could the gaseous product be tested for?

11 The fermentation lock has two purposes in this activity. What are they?

(i)

(ii)

12 During the activity the liquid seems to foam up. What causes this?

13 Towards the end of the activity the rate of foam production seems to slow down. Give a reason for this.

14 During the activity a rise in temperature was noticed in the reaction vessel. Give a reason for this.

_____

15 How did you know that fermentation was no longer happening?

_____

_____

16 Explain how the breathalyser test works.

_____

_____

_____

17 Name a substance produced in muscle during anaerobic respiration.

_____

18 Name a substance produced in aerobic respiration that is not produced during anaerobic respiration.

_____

Examination note

This activity was examined in Section B of the Leaving Cert Biology Exam in **2012** (HL) and **2004** (HL).
It also appeared in Section C **2012** (OL) Q14a, **2009** (OL) Q15b, **2007** (OL) Q12c, **2006** (OL) Q13c and
2005 (HL) Q11c.

Chapter 7 | Osmosis

Activity 14 | To demonstrate osmosis

Theory:

Osmosis is the movement of water from a dilute solution to a more concentrated solution through a semi-permeable (selectively permeable) membrane. In this experiment, Visking tubing is used because its behaviour closely resembles that of the cell membrane. To estimate the process of osmosis, we investigate the change in mass of the tube of sucrose and also the change in turgidity of the solution in the Visking tubing (i.e. the tubing becomes swollen).

Materials:

- Visking tubing
- 80% sucrose solution
- Distilled water
- Two 250cm³ beakers
- Two glass rods
- Electronic balance
- Scissors
- Blotting paper

Procedure:

1. Soak 20cm of Visking tubing in distilled water until soft.
2. Cut the tube in two.
3. Tie a knot at one end of each tube.
4. Transfer 20cm³ of the sucrose solution into one tube. Tie off and dry.
5. Transfer 20cm³ of distilled water into the other tube. Tie off and dry.
6. Find the mass of each of the sealed tubes.
7. Place in distilled water supported by a glass rod (to prevent leakage from the ends of the tubes) as shown in the diagram.
8. Leave for 15 minutes.
9. Dry the outside of each of the tubes and find the mass of each of them.
10. Note also the turgidity of the Visking tubing.

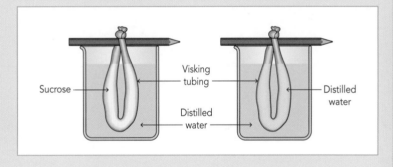

STUDENT REPORT Activity **14**

Title: _____

_____ *Date:* _____

Procedure:

_____
_____
_____
_____
_____
_____
_____
_____
_____
_____
_____
_____
_____
_____
_____
_____

Results:

	Mass before	Mass after	Change in mass	Change in appearance (turgidity)
Sucrose solution				
Distilled water				

Diagram:

Risks:

_____

_____

_____

_____

Risk management:

_____

_____

_____

Skills:

_____

_____

_____

_____

Skill application:

_____

_____

_____

Conclusions/comments:

_____

_____

_____

_____

Signature:

_____

Activity **14** Questions

1 Define osmosis.

_____

_____

2 Distinguish between osmosis and diffusion.

_____

_____

3 What is Visking tubing?

_____

_____

4 In this activity, what part of the cell structure does Visking tubing represent?

_____

5 What does semi-permeable mean?

_____

6 Name a biological structure that is:

Semi-permeable _____

Fully permeable _____

Impermeable _____

7 Explain each of the following terms:

Solute _____

_____

Solution _____

_____

8 In this activity, why are the tied ends of the Visking tubing kept out of the water?

_____

_____

9 What step should be taken before weighing each 'tube' of Visking tubing and why?

_____

_____

10 Was there a change in the mass and/or appearance of the 'tube' of water at the end of the activity? Explain.

_____

_____

11 Was there a change in the mass and/or appearance of the 'tube' of sucrose at the end of the activity? Explain.

_____

_____

12 How were you able to tell that osmosis had taken place in this activity?

_____

_____

13 If the 'tubes' of sucrose and water had been placed in sucrose solution instead of distilled water, would the results have been different? Explain.

_____

_____

14 Name the osmoregulatory organs in the human body.

_____

Examination note

This activity was examined in Section B of the Leaving Cert Biology Exam in **2012** (HL), **2009** (OL) and **2005** (OL). It also appeared in Section C in **2011** (HL) Q14c, **2008** (HL) Q14c and **2008** (OL) Q15a.

Chapter **8** | DNA

Activity 15 To isolate DNA from plant tissue

Theory:

DNA is extracted from onion bulb cells, which have a high number of meristematic cells and thus a large concentration of DNA present. The steps taken in this procedure are all designed to release the DNA from the nuclei of the growing cells.

- **Chopping the cells** – breaks down cell walls and membranes.
- **Adding washing-up liquid** – disturbs cell membrane lipid bilayer and causes cell membranes to clump together.
- **Adding salt** – stops the attraction between DNA and cell proteins and causes the DNA to clump together.
- **Heating the mixture for 15 minutes at 60°C** – stops the activity of cell enzymes, which break down DNA.
- **Cooling the mixture** – stops any further enzyme activity.
- **Blending** – causes further breakdown of cell walls and membranes.
- **Filtering** – removes debris. Use a coffee filter paper, otherwise the process is too slow.
- **Adding protease enzyme** – breaks down proteins associated with DNA. (Note that kiwi fruit produces its own protease).
- **Adding ethanol** – DNA is insoluble in cold ethanol and precipitates at the water–ethanol interface.

Materials:

- Medium-sized onion (or kiwi fruit)
- $10cm^3$ washing-up liquid
- 3g salt
- $100cm^3$ distilled water
- Ice bath
- Food blender
- Coffee filter paper
- Protease solution (e.g. pepsin, contact lens cleaner)
- Ice-cold ethanol

Procedure:

1 Mix the water, salt and washing-up liquid in a $250cm^3$ beaker.
2 Chop the onion into small pieces and add to the mixture.
3 Place the mixture in a water bath at 60°C for 15 minutes.
4 Place in ice bath for 5 minutes.
5 Blend for 3 seconds.
6 Filter into a measuring cylinder using coffee filter paper.
7 Pour $6cm^3$ of the onion filtrate into a test tube.
8 Add 4 drops of protease enzyme.
9 Carefully add $9cm^3$ ice-cold ethanol down the side of the test tube.
10 Using an inoculating loop, extract the strands of DNA which appear, and allow to dry.

Procedure:

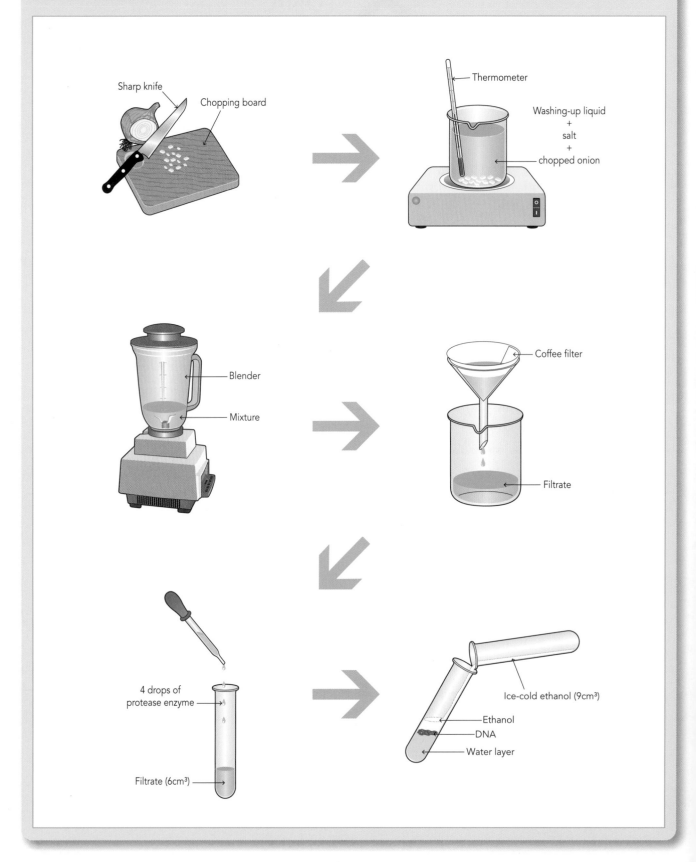

STUDENT REPORT | **Activity** | **15**

Title: _____

_____ *Date:* _____

Procedure:

_____
_____
_____
_____
_____
_____
_____
_____
_____
_____
_____
_____
_____
_____
_____
_____
_____
_____
_____
_____
_____

Results:

_____
_____
_____
_____

Diagram:

Risks:
_____
_____

Risk management:
_____
_____

Skills:
_____
_____

Skill application:
_____
_____

Conclusions/comments:
_____
_____

Signature:
_____

Activity 15 Questions

1 Why is the onion/kiwi fruit chopped?

_____

_____

2 Why is washing-up liquid added to the mixture?

_____

_____

3 Why is salt added to the mixture?

_____

_____

4 Why is the mixture heated to 60°C for 15 minutes?

_____

_____

5 Why is the mixture cooled?

_____

_____

6 Why is the mixture blended?

_____

_____

7 Why is the mixture blended for no more than 3 seconds?

_____

_____

8 Why is the mixture filtered?

_____

_____

9 Why is coffee filter paper used?

_____

10 What is a protease enzyme?

_____

11 Why is a protease enzyme added to the filtered solution?

_____

12 If pepsin or trypsin are not available in the lab, contact lens cleaner or meat tenderiser can be used to carry out this activity. Give a reason for this.

_____

_____

13 Why is ice-cold ethanol added to the solution?

14 What is observed when the ice-cold ethanol is added?

15 Why is a bactericidal washing-up liquid not used in this activity?

16 Where exactly does the DNA sample appear in the ethanol/water mixture?

Examination note

This activity was examined in Section B of the Leaving Cert Biology Exam in **2011** (HL), **2010** (HL and OL), **2006** (HL) and **2005** (HL). It also appeared in **2010** Section C (HL)10c.

Chapter **9** | Fungi

To investigate the growth of leaf yeast using malt agar plates

Theory:

Yeasts grow naturally on many leaves. Yeasts are found on the under surface of the leaf where sugars exude through the stomata. The number of yeast cells present on a leaf is often an indication of the level of pollutants such as SO_2 in the atmosphere. High SO_2 levels reduce yeast populations.

Lichen population numbers could also be used in this type of investigation. Leaves from deciduous trees such as privet, ash, oak, sycamore, hawthorn, lilac and red alder can be used. Leaves like cherry, alder and clover must not be used as they emit cyanide, which poisons the yeast. Ideally, use leaves from a number of habitats (e.g. city, suburban and country) to give an accurate assessment of how changes in the environment affect the number of yeast colonies.

The procedures in this experiment involve aseptic techniques, which means the exclusion of any possibility of infection by unwanted micro-organisms.

Notes:

- This activity is best carried out in September to allow for sufficient levels of yeast colonies to grow.
- Carry out the activity on the day the leaf samples are collected.

Materials:

- Fresh leaves
- Two sterile malt agar plates
- Adhesive tape (parafilm)
- Vaseline
- Forceps
- Scissors
- Inoculating loop
- Bunsen burner
- Distilled water
- Disinfectant

Procedure:

1 Collect some leaves from an outdoor plant. Note the name of the plant. (See above for some ideas.)
2 Wash your hands.
3 Swab down the work surface using disinfectant.
4 Sterilise the forceps, scissors and inoculating loop by heating in a Bunsen burner flame and cooling in distilled water (or place in disinfectant).
5 Using the forceps, pick up one of the leaves and cut it into a few small pieces with the scissors.
6 Using the inoculating loop, place a small blob of Vaseline on the upper surface of the leaf pieces.
7 Carefully open the lid of one of the agar plates (as short a distance and for as short a time as possible) and attach the leaf pieces to the under surface of the lid.
8 Close the agar plate, seal with adhesive tape and label 'Experimental Plate'.
9 Open the lid of the other agar plate and place some Vaseline on the under surface of the lid using the same aseptic techniques as before.
10 Close the agar plate, seal with adhesive tape and label 'Control Plate'.
11 Leave the plates in an upright position for 24 hours to allow the yeast to fall on to the agar.
12 Invert and incubate the plates for 3 days at 25–30°C.
13 View the results.
14 At the end of the experiment, dispose of the agar plates carefully. (Sterilise in an autoclave for 15 minutes or in disinfectant for 24 hours and then put in a bin.)

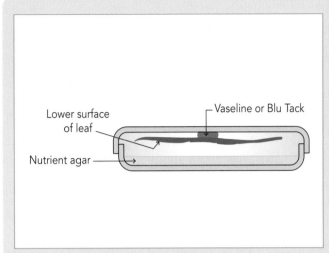

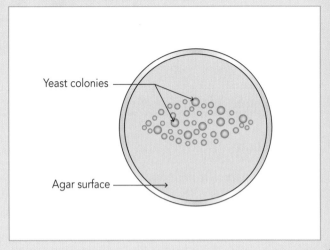

STUDENT REPORT Activity **16**

Title: _____

_____ *Date:* _____

Procedure:

_____
_____
_____
_____
_____
_____
_____
_____
_____
_____
_____
_____
_____
_____
_____
_____

Results:

Plate	Appearance of colonies
Experimental	
Control	

Diagram:

Risks:

Risk management:

Skills:

Skill application:

Conclusions/comments:

Signature:

Activity 16 Questions

1 To which kingdom do yeasts belong? _____

2 Yeasts are eukaryotic organisms. Distinguish between the terms *prokaryotic* and *eukaryotic*.
_____
_____

3 Name a fungus, other than yeast, that you have studied during your course.
_____

4 Distinguish between aseptic and sterile techniques in relation to microbiology.
_____
_____

5 What aseptic techniques are used in this activity?
_____
_____

6 Name the type of leaf used in this activity. _____

7 Describe how the leaf was collected. _____
_____

8 Leaves such as clover cannot be used in this activity. Why? _____
_____

9 Name the container in which the leaf yeast is grown. _____

10 It is necessary to use a nutrient medium in order to grow leaf yeast. What is a nutrient medium and why
is it used? _____
_____

11 Name the nutrient medium used in this activity.
_____

12 Why are the leaves attached at the upper surface to the lid of the agar plate?
_____

13 Why are the agar plates left to stand for 24 hours before being inverted?
_____

14 What control is used in this activity?
_____

15 Why are the agar plates (a) incubated at 25°C–30°C; (b) incubated for 3 days; (c) inverted; and (d) sealed?

(a) _____ (b) _____

(c) _____ (d) _____

16 How long does it take for the leaf yeast to appear?
_____

Examination note

This activity was examined in Section B of the Leaving Cert Biology Exam in **2012** (HL), **2011** (OL), **2010** (HL), **2008** (OL), **2007** (HL) and **2005** (HL).

Chapter **10** Dicot Stem

Activity 17 To prepare and examine a transverse section (TS) of a dicot stem

Theory:

The purpose of this activity is to investigate and identify the tissues of a transverse section of a dicot stem. The stem is differentiated into three distinct tissues:

1 **Dermal tissue** forms a protective layer against water and bacteria. It consists of an outer waxy layer called the **cuticle**, below which is the **epidermis**. To aid gaseous exchange, this tissue may also contain stomata.

2 **Ground tissue** makes up most of the tissue of the stem. It may act as storage, support or photosynthetic tissue.

3 **Vascular tissue** consists of the **phloem**, which transports food material, and the **xylem**, which transports water and minerals up the stem.

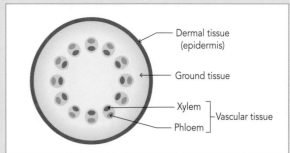

Materials:

- Dicotyledonous stems (e.g. busy lizzy)
- Microscope
- Microscope slides
- Cover slips
- Mounted needle
- Petri dish
- Backed blade or microtome
- Small paintbrush
- Dropper
- Absorbent paper
- Stains

Procedure:

1 Set up the microscope.

2 Place a drop of water on a slide.

3 Wet the blade to give a clean cut.

4 Cut a short piece of stem between the nodes using the wet blade. Cut across the stem at right angles away from the body, to get very thin transverse sections.

5 To prevent damaging very young or soft stems and to achieve a very thin cut, an elder pith or a carrot cut lengthways and hollowed out can be used for support. A microtome can also be used to get a thinner section.

6 Repeat several times and put all the sections into the Petri dish containing water.

7 Transfer the thinnest section into the drop of water on the slide using the paintbrush.

8 Place a cover slip at the edge of the water at an angle of 45° to the slide.

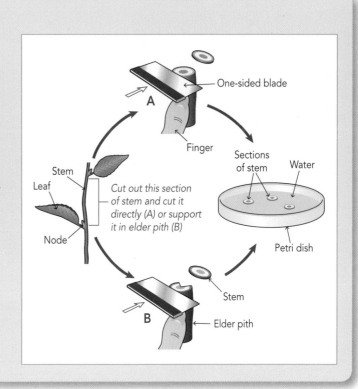

Procedure:

9 Slowly lower the cover slip onto the slide, supporting with a mounted needle to avoid trapping air bubbles.

10 Dry the slide with absorbent paper.

11 Repeat steps 2–10, this time placing the sections in some stain, such as iodine (stains starch blue-black), aniline sulfate (stains lignin yellow) or Schultz's solution (stains cellulose purple), for 5 minutes.

12 Examine the slide under the microscope.

13 Draw labelled diagrams of what you see at medium power (x100) and at high power (x400).

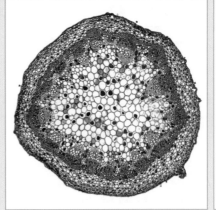
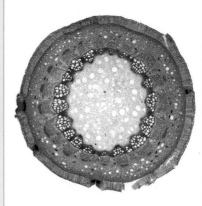

STUDENT REPORT **Activity 17**

Title: _____

_____ Date: _____

Procedure:

_____
_____
_____
_____
_____
_____
_____
_____
_____
_____
_____
_____
_____
_____
_____
_____
_____
_____
_____
_____

Results:

Medium power	High power

Risks:
_____
_____

Risk management:
_____
_____

Skills:
_____
_____
_____

Skill application:
_____
_____
_____

Conclusions/comments:
_____
_____
_____

Signature:

Activity 17 Questions

1 List three differences between monocot and dicot plants.

_____

_____

_____

2 In this activity, why are herbaceous stems preferred to woody stems?

_____

3 For what purpose may a carrot or an elder pith be used in this activity?

_____

4 What is meant by the term _transverse section_?

_____

5 Why is it desirable to cut the sections as thinly as possible?

_____

_____

6 Why are the sections placed in water?

_____

_____

7 Why is the stem cut between the nodes?

_____

_____

8 Using a scalpel or blade can be very hazardous. How can the risk of injury be minimised in this activity?

_____

_____

9 Why are only very thin sections used when viewing sections under a light microscope?

_____

_____

10 Vascular tissue is one of the tissues identified. Name and give the function of the two transport tissues in vascular tissue.

(i) _____

(ii) _____

11 Name the two other tissues that are identified in the section.

(i) _____

(ii) _____

12 Name a stain that could be used in this activity. _____

13 What material is stained by the stain mentioned above?

_____

Examination note

This activity was examined in Section B of the Leaving Cert Biology Exam in **2011** (HL), **2010** (OL), **2009** (HL) and **2004** (HL). It also appeared in Section C **2006** (HL) Q14c.

Chapter **11** | The Heart

Activity **18** To dissect, display and identify the parts of a sheep's heart

Theory:

The human heart is a four-chambered structure. The left side, which pumps blood to the whole body, is divided into the left atrium, which receives oxygenated blood from the lungs via the pulmonary vein, and the left ventricle, which pumps newly oxygenated blood through the aorta to the whole body. For this reason, the left side of the heart, in particular the left ventricle, is much larger than the right.

The right side of the heart receives deoxygenated blood from the body. This blood flows through the vena cava into the right atrium, and the right ventricle pumps the deoxygenated blood to the lungs via the pulmonary artery.

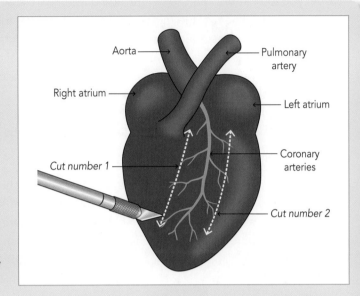

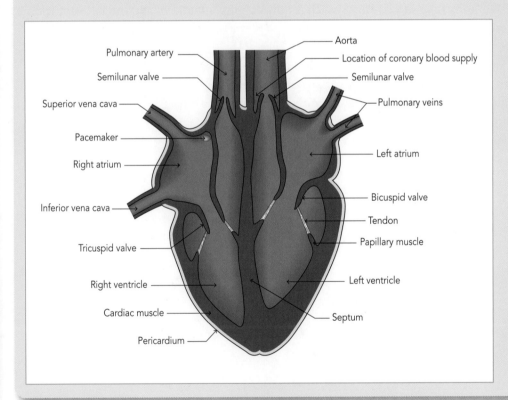

Materials:

- Sheep's heart
- Dissecting board
- Scalpel
- Scissors
- Seeker
- Flag labels
- Disposable gloves
- Absorbent paper
- Disinfectant

Procedure:

(a) Identification

1 Wash the heart with cold water, drain it and dry it with absorbent paper.
2 Place the heart on the dissecting board so that the front (ventral) side is facing up. (The front of the heart is more curved than the back; and there is a groove on the front of the heart that extends diagonally downwards from the left side of the broad end where a coronary vessel is located.)
3 As you look at the heart, the right side of the heart is on your left.
4 Note the thickness of the muscle wall on each side of the heart.
5 Locate the four chambers of the heart (right atrium, right ventricle, left atrium, left ventricle).
6 Locate the four main blood vessels at the broad end of the heart (vena cava, pulmonary artery, pulmonary vein, aorta). Insert the seeker or your finger through the arteries to help you identify them.
7 Note the thickness of the wall of each vessel.
8 Observe the coronary blood vessels located in the wall of the heart.
9 Draw a labelled diagram of the external structure of the heart.

(b) Dissection

10 Carefully cut from the right atrium down to the tip of the right ventricle. Keep the cut as close as possible to the centre (the septum). Repeat for the left side of the heart.
11 Open the heart to examine its internal structure. If there is any blood inside, rinse it out.
12 Note the different sizes of the chambers.
13 Locate the septum, a thick muscular wall that separates the right and left sides of the heart.
14 Locate the tricuspid valve, consisting of three flaps, which is between the right atrium and the right ventricle.
15 Locate the bicuspid valve, consisting of two flaps, which is between the left atrium and the left ventricle.
16 Note the tendons (chordae tendinae) connecting the bicuspid and tricuspid valves to papillary muscles in the wall of the heart.
17 Using the scalpel, cut upwards from the right ventricle and observe the semilunar valves in the pulmonary artery. Note the three half moon-shaped flaps of this valve.
18 Repeat for the left ventricle to cut open the aorta and observe its semilunar valves.
19 Find two small openings at the base of the aorta. These lead into the coronary arteries.
20 Flag label the parts identified and draw a labelled diagram of the internal structure of the heart.
21 Wash and sterilise the dissecting instruments and board after use.

STUDENT REPORT   Activity   **18**

Title: _____

_____ *Date:* _____

Procedure:

_____
_____
_____
_____
_____
_____
_____
_____
_____
_____
_____
_____
_____
_____
_____
_____
_____
_____
_____
_____
_____
_____
_____
_____
_____
_____

Results:

Chamber	Size (small/large)	Wall (thick/thin)
Right atrium		
Right ventricle		
Left atrium		
Left ventricle		

Blood vessels	Wall (thick/thin)
Vena cava	
Pulmonary artery	
Pulmonary vein	
Aorta	

Valve type	Number of flaps
Bicuspid	
Tricuspid	
Semilunar	

Diagram:
External structure

Diagram:
Internal structure

Risks:
_____
_____

Risk management:
_____
_____

Skills:
_____
_____

Skill application:
_____
_____

Conclusions/comments:
_____
_____

Signature:
_____

Activity 18 Questions

1 How can you distinguish between the ventral (front) and dorsal (back) surfaces of the heart?

_____

_____

2 How can you distinguish between the right and left sides of the heart?

_____

_____

3 Four main arteries are attached to the heart. How can you tell which are arteries and which are veins?

_____

_____

4 What is the name of the wall of muscle that separates the right and left sides of the heart?

_____

5 What is the name of the blood vessel that supplies the heart tissue itself with food and oxygen? Where is the origin of this blood vessel?

_____

_____

6 Distinguish between pulmonary circulation and systemic circulation.

_____

_____

7 Name one part of the circulatory system where oxygen-rich blood is found.

_____

8 Name one part of the circulatory system where oxygen-poor blood is found.

_____

9 What instrument is used to dissect the heart?

_____

10 When dissecting a heart, where should the first incision be made?

_____

11 What structure on the surface of the heart can be used as a guideline to the location of the septum?

_____

12 Which chamber of the heart has the greatest amount of muscle in its wall?

_____

13 In which chamber is the pacemaker located?

_____

14 Where in the heart is papillary muscle located?

_____

15 Why is the muscle wall on the left side of the heart thicker than that on the right side?

_____

16 State one way in which heart muscle differs from other muscles in the body.

_____

17 Where are the semilunar valves located and how did you expose them during this dissection?

_____

_____

18 Name the cavity in the body where the heart and lungs are located.

_____

Examination note

This activity was examined in Section B of the Leaving Cert Biology Exam in **2012** (HL), **2010** (HL), **2006** (OL) and **2004** (HL).

Activity 19a To investigate the effect of exercise on human pulse rate

Theory:

The human body needs a constant supply of oxygen so that each cell can respire and produce energy. During exercise, the body needs an increased supply of oxygen to meet the demands of the working muscles. As the muscles respire, they produce CO_2 as a waste product. An increase in the levels of CO_2 in the blood causes the medulla oblongata in the brain to trigger an increase in both heart rate and breathing rate.

Note: The pulse rate in beats per minute is the same as the heart rate in beats per minute.

Note: This activity must not be undertaken by anyone with health problems.

Materials:

- Stopwatch/pulse rate monitor

Procedure:

1 Work in pairs (one person as subject and one person recording results).
2 Pulse rate is recorded by taking the number of pulses in 15 seconds and multiplying this figure by 4.
3 Identify a strong pulse in the neck or wrist of the subject.
4 Place the subject in a sitting position. Measure the pulse rate three times and calculate the average.
5 Have the subject stand and immediately measure the pulse rate.
6 Have the subject walk slowly for 5 minutes and immediately measure the pulse rate.
7 Wait for the pulse rate to return to normal. Have the subject exercise strenuously for 2 minutes and then immediately measure the pulse rate.
8 Measure the pulse rate every minute until it returns to the resting rate.
9 Record your results in the table below.
10 Plot heart rate against time.

Note: The thumb should not be used when measuring pulse rate because the thumb has its own pulse.

STUDENT REPORT | Activity **19a**

Title: _____

_____ *Date:* _____

Procedure:

Results:

Activity		Pulse rate (bpm)
Resting:	Reading 1	
	Reading 2	
	Reading 3	
Average resting rate		
Standing		
Slow walk		
Strenuous exercise		
After exercise:	1 minute	
	2 minutes	
	3 minutes	
	4 minutes	
	5 minutes	
	6 minutes	
	7 minutes	
	8 minutes	
	9 minutes	
	10 minutes	

Graph:

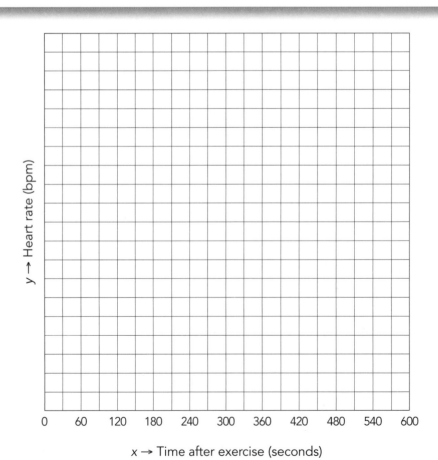

Risks:

_____
_____
_____
_____

Risk management:

_____
_____
_____
_____

Skills:

_____
_____
_____
_____

Skill application:

_____
_____
_____
_____

Conclusions/comments:

_____
_____
_____
_____
_____

Signature:

_____

Activity **19a** Questions

1 What is the average human resting heart rate? _____

2 At the start of this activity, the subject is asked to sit down for a few minutes. Explain the purpose of this.

_____

_____

3 How is pulse rate measured in this activity?

_____

4 In what type of blood vessel can a pulse be detected?

_____

5 Where in a human body can a pulse be easily detected?

_____

6 Why should you never use your thumb to measure pulse rate?

_____

7 Why is the resting pulse rate measured three times?

_____

8 After exercise, why is the pulse rate only measured once?

_____

9 What happens to a person's heart rate when they stand up and why?

_____

_____

10 Why do top athletes have very low resting heart rates?

_____

11 If it takes a person a long time to return to their resting heart rate after exercise, what does this indicate about their level of fitness?

_____

_____

12 Where is the electrical energy in the heart generated?

_____

13 Briefly describe the nervous pathway through the heart.

_____

_____

14 In order to control heart rate, the brain measures the blood level of which gas?

_____

15 What part of the brain controls heart rate? _____

16 Name a hormone that increases heart rate and state where it is produced.

_____

Examination note

This activity was examined in Section B of the Leaving Cert Biology Exam in **2012** (OL), **2011** (HL), **2008** (OL) and **2004** (OL).

Activity **19b** To investigate the effect of exercise on human breathing rate

Note: This activity must not be undertaken by anyone with health problems.

Materials:

- Stopwatch/respirometer

Procedure:

1 Work in pairs (one person as subject and one person recording results).

2 Breathing rate is recorded by taking the number of breaths in a minute. Breathing in and out is taken as one breath.

3 Place the subject in a sitting position. Measure the breathing rate three times and calculate the average.

4 Have the subject stand and immediately measure the breathing rate.

5 Have the subject walk slowly for 5 minutes and immediately measure the breathing rate.

6 Wait for the breathing rate to return to normal and have the subject exercise strenuously for 5 minutes. Immediately measure the breathing rate.

7 Measure the breathing rate every minute until it returns to (or below) the resting rate.

8 Record your results in the table below.

9 Plot breathing rate against time.

Title: _____

_____ Date: _____

Procedure:

_____
_____
_____
_____
_____
_____
_____
_____
_____
_____
_____
_____
_____
_____
_____
_____
_____
_____
_____
_____
_____
_____
_____
_____
_____
_____

Results:

Activity		Breathing rate
Resting:	Reading 1	
	Reading 2	
	Reading 3	
Average resting rate		
Standing		
Slow walk		
Strenuous exercise		
After exercise:	1 minute	
	2 minutes	
	3 minutes	
	4 minutes	
	5 minutes	
	6 minutes	
	7 minutes	
	8 minutes	
	9 minutes	
	10 minutes	

Graph:

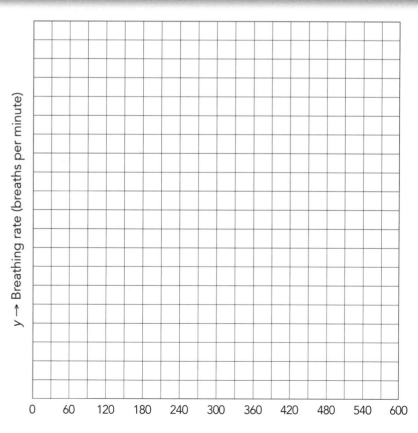

Risks:

_____

_____

_____

_____

Risk management:

_____

_____

_____

_____

Skills:

_____

_____

_____

_____

Skill application:

_____

_____

_____

_____

Conclusions/comments:

_____

_____

_____

_____

Signature:

_____

Activity **19b** Questions

1 What is the average human resting breathing rate?

_____

2 At the start of this activity, the subject is asked to sit down for a few minutes. Explain the purpose of this.

_____

_____

3 How is breathing rate measured in this activity?

_____

4 Why is the resting breathing rate measured three times?

_____

5 What happens to a person's breathing rate when they stand up and why?

_____

_____

6 Why is it necessary to wait for the subject's resting breathing rate to return to normal before having them undertake strenuous exercise?

_____

7 What factors are kept constant during this activity?

_____

8 What factors are varied during this activity?

_____

9 What effect does exercise have on breathing rate?

_____

10 Explain why exercise affects breathing rate.

_____

_____

11 Does this investigation give the same result for both fit and non-fit people? Give a reason for your answer.

_____

_____

12 Distinguish between breathing and respiration.

_____

13 In order to control breathing rate, the brain measures the blood level of which gas?

_____

14 What part of the brain controls breathing rate?

_____

Examination note

This activity was examined in Section B of the Leaving Cert Biology Exam in **2012** (OL), **2008** (OL) and **2004** (OL).

Chapter 12 | Plant Growth and Seed Germination

Theory:

Plants respond to various stimuli through processes called tropisms. These growth responses can be positive or negative. These responses are controlled by chemicals in the plant called growth regulators. One such growth regulator is IAA (indole acetic acid). At high concentrations, IAA promotes stem growth; at low concentrations it promotes root growth. In this experiment, the student first makes a serial dilution of a stock solution of IAA. These solutions are made because it is impossible to weigh out very small amounts of the chemical.

Materials:

- Radish seeds (or other suitable seeds)
- Eight Petri dishes
- Diluted solutions of IAA 10^2, 10^1, 10^0, 10^{-1}, 10^{-2}, 10^{-3}, 10^{-4} ppm. These solutions will be made by serial dilutions – Procedure (a)
- Distilled water
- Circular acetate grids*
- Filter papers
- Cotton wool
- Disposable gloves
- Eight graduated droppers (labelled with the appropriate concentration for use)
- Eight bottles (labelled with the appropriate concentration for use)
- Sealing tape

* Gridded acetate is obtained by photocopying graph paper on to acetate. This is cut to fit the Petri dish.

Procedure:

(a): Making a 10^2 ppm (parts per million) solution of IAA and serial dilution to 10^{-4} ppm

1. Dissolve 0.1g of IAA powder in $10cm^3$ of ethanol. IAA is sparingly soluble in water but soluble in ethanol.
2. Make this solution up to 1 litre with distilled water.
3. Label eight $20cm^3$ screw-cap bottles as follows: 10^2, 10^1, 10^0, 10^{-1}, 10^{-2}, 10^{-3}, 10^{-4}, distilled water (control).
4. Label eight droppers as above.
5. Place $10cm^3$ of the stock solution in the bottle labelled 10^2.
6. Using the correct dropper, remove $1cm^3$ of the solution above and place in the bottle labelled 10^1.
7. Dilute this solution with $9cm^3$ of distilled water to $10cm^3$.
8. Repeat steps 6–7 to make subsequent solutions.
9. Remove $1cm^3$ from the bottle labelled 10^{-4} to ensure that all bottles contain $9cm^3$ of solution.
10. Finally place $9cm^3$ of distilled water in the last bottle as a **control**.

Procedure:

(b): Setting up Petri dishes containing seeds

1 Label eight Petri dishes according to their concentration.
2 Place a circular acetate in the lid of each dish.
3 Place five radish seeds along a line in the grid.
4 Place a filter paper over the seeds.
5 Moisten the paper with 2cm³ of the appropriate solution using the correct dropper.
6 Now add enough cotton wool to fill the dish.
7 Moisten this cotton wool with 7cm³ of the same concentration solution.
8 Cover with the base of the dish and seal with sealing tape.
9 Continue with this procedure for each dish.
10 Leave the dishes in a standing position in a warm place for three days.
11 Record your results in the charts below.

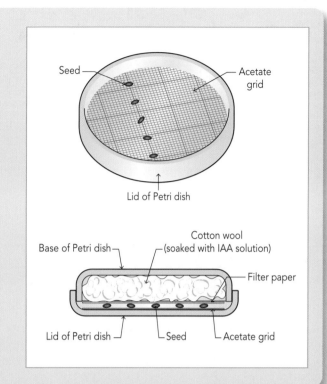

STUDENT REPORT **Activity** **20**

Title: _____

_____ *Date:* _____

Procedure:

_____
_____
_____
_____
_____
_____
_____
_____
_____
_____
_____
_____
_____
_____
_____

Procedure:

_____

_____

_____

_____

_____

_____

_____

_____

_____

_____

_____

_____

_____

_____

_____

_____

_____

Results:

$$\% \text{ stimulation} = \frac{(\text{average length} - \text{average length of control})}{\text{average length of control}} \times 100$$

Root length:

IAA conc.	Seed 1	Seed 2	Seed 3	Seed 4	Seed 5	Total length	Average length	% stimulation
Control								
10^{-4}								
10^{-3}								
10^{-2}								
10^{-1}								
10^{0}								
10^{1}								
10^{2}								

Results:

Shoot length:

IAA conc.	Seed 1	Seed 2	Seed 3	Seed 4	Seed 5	Total length	Average length	% stimulation
Control								
10^{-4}								
10^{-3}								
10^{-2}								
10^{-1}								
10^{0}								
10^{1}								
10^{2}								

	IAA concentration
Best shoot stimulation	
Best root stimulation	

12 **Graph:**

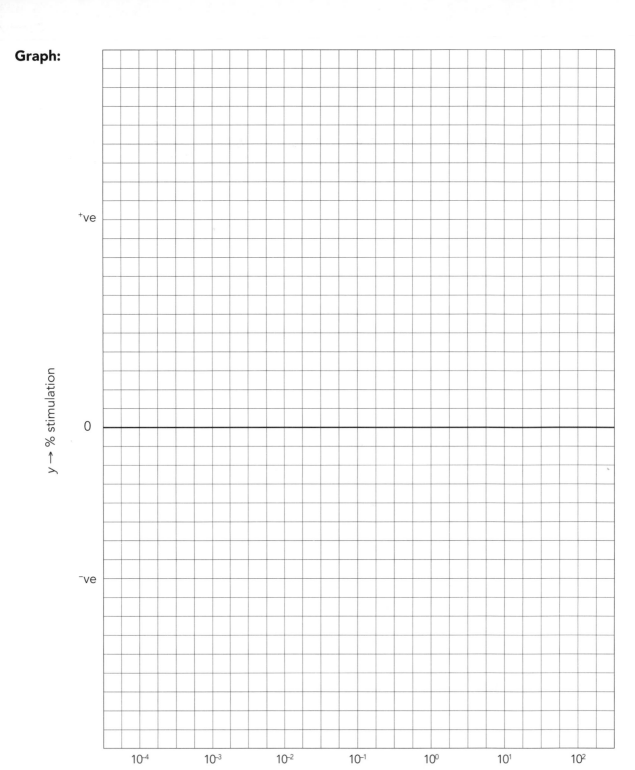

Diagram:

(a) Serial dilution

Diagram:

(b) Preparing Petri dishes

Risks:

_____
_____
_____
_____

Risk management:

_____
_____
_____
_____

Skills:

_____
_____
_____
_____

Skill application:

_____
_____
_____
_____

Conclusions/comments:

_____
_____
_____
_____

Signature:

Activity **20** Questions

1 What are plant growth regulators?

_____

2 What are auxins?

_____

_____

3 List four functions of auxins.

(i) _____ (iii) _____

(ii) _____ (iv) _____

4 Name a plant growth regulator that inhibits growth.

_____

5 Give one function of this plant growth inhibitor.

_____

_____

6 What do the letters IAA stand for? _____

7 What is the concentration of the stock solution of IAA that is used in this activity?

_____

8 Why are serial dilutions used in biological experiments?

_____

_____

_____

9 Why are acetate grids placed in each Petri dish?

_____

_____

10 What types of seeds are used in this activity?

_____

11 How are these seeds treated in order to get them to germinate?

_____

_____

12 How many seeds are placed in each Petri dish and why is that number of seeds used?

_____

_____

13 Name one use of plant growth promoters in horticulture.

_____

14 Give one use of plant growth inhibitors.

_____

Examination note

This activity was examined in Section B of the Leaving Cert Biology Exam in **2010** (HL), **2008** (HL) and **2006** (HL).

Activity 21 — To investigate the effect of water, oxygen and temperature on germination

Theory:

Germination is the growth of the plant embryo. After dispersal, the seed first goes through a period of dormancy to ensure that the young plant does not start to grow in unfavourable conditions. After the seed has completed this period of dormancy, it requires the following to germinate: **oxygen** for respiration; **water** to allow the seed cover (testa) to soften; and sufficient **heat** to facilitate respiration.

Materials:

- 40 radish seeds
  (other seeds, e.g. peas, broad beans, can be used)
- Distilled water
- Anaerobic kit
  (covering the seeds with boiled water and oil can also be used as an anaerobic apparatus)
- 4 Petri dishes
- Thermometers
- Fridge
- Cotton wool

Procedure:

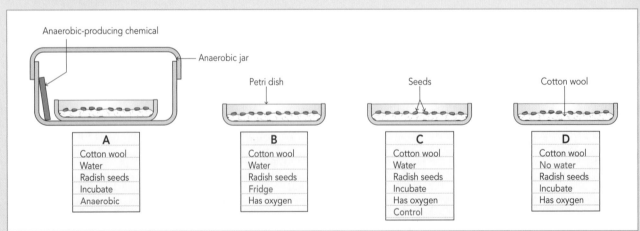

1. Label the Petri dishes A, B, C and D.
2. Place cotton wool in each dish.
3. Moisten A, B and C with distilled water. Do not add any water to D.
4. Place 10 seeds in each dish.
5. Place A in the anaerobic jar (no oxygen).
6. Place B in a fridge (no heat).
7. Leave A, C and D in a warm place (20–25°C).
8. Leave the dishes for three days and record whether or not germination has occurred.

STUDENT REPORT Activity **21**

Title: _____

_____ *Date:* _____

Procedure:

_____

_____

_____

_____

_____

_____

_____

_____

_____

_____

_____

_____

_____

_____

_____

_____

_____

_____

_____

_____

_____

_____

_____

_____

_____

_____

_____

Results:

Seeds	A Cotton wool Water Radish seeds Incubate *Anaerobic*	B Cotton wool Water Radish seeds *Fridge* Has oxygen	C Cotton wool Water Radish seeds Incubate Has oxygen *Control*	D Cotton wool *No water* Radish seeds Incubate Has oxygen
Appearance of plumule				
Appearance of radicle				

Diagram:

Risks:

_____
_____
_____
_____

Risk management:

_____
_____
_____
_____

Skills:

_____
_____
_____
_____

Skill application:

_____
_____
_____
_____

Conclusions/comments:

_____
_____
_____
_____

Signature:

_____

Activity **21** Questions

1 What is meant by dormancy in seeds?

_____

2 Give two benefits of seeds being dormant for a period.

_____

_____

3 What is meant by germination of seeds?

_____

4 Name the type of seeds used in this activity.

_____

5 In this activity, which seeds are used as a control?

_____

6 Why are 10 seeds placed in each Petri dish?

_____

7 Name the biochemical process that occurs during germination that requires oxygen.

_____

8 How is the oxygen removed from dish A?

_____

9 How is dish B deprived of a suitable temperature?

_____

10 What is observed that indicates that germination has taken place?

_____

11 Why are dishes B, C and D left uncovered?

_____

12 Why are dishes A, C and D kept at 20–25°C?

_____

13 Beans, peas, lentils and soya beans form an important part of a vegetarian's diet. Give a reason for this.

_____

_____

14 In which dish do the seeds show the best rate of germination?

_____

15 What do the results tell you about the optimum conditions for germination?

_____

Examination note

This activity was examined in Section B of the Leaving Cert Biology Exam in **2008** (OL), **2006** (HL and OL) and **2005** (OL). It also appeared in Section C **2004** (OL) Q14c.

Activity 22 To use starch agar or skimmed milk plates to show digestive activity during germination

Theory:

During germination the growing seed carries out respiration. The nutrients required are stored in the seed itself as carbohydrates, fats or proteins. In endospermic seeds, the food is stored in the endosperm; in nonendospermic seeds, the cotyledons are the food store. To digest the stored food to simpler forms, the seed uses enzymes.

Materials:

- Broad bean seeds
- Two sterile starch agar plates*
- Mild disinfectant
- Forceps
- Sharp blade
- Incubator
- Chopping board
- Iodine solution/biuret reagent

* Skimmed milk agar plates may also be used to show the activity of peptidase enzymes during germination. Protein may be tested for, using biuret reagent.

Procedure:

1 Soak eight broad bean seeds for 2–3 days.
2 Sterilise all glassware and equipment before use.
3 Place four seeds in boiling water for 20 minutes to kill them (and denature their enzymes).
4 Sterilise the remaining seeds in a mild disinfectant.
5 Split all the seeds in half lengthways, using a sharp blade.
6 Place the cut, unboiled seeds face down onto the agar in one of the plates. The lid of the plate should be barely open.
7 Replace the lid.
8 Repeat this procedure for the boiled seeds.
9 Place the Petri dishes in an incubator at 20°C for 2 days.
10 Test both plates for starch using iodine solution.
11 Record the results.

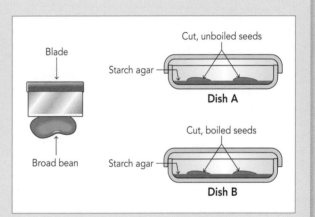

STUDENT REPORT Activity **22**

Title: _____

_____ *Date:* _____

Procedure:

_____
_____
_____
_____
_____
_____
_____
_____
_____
_____
_____
_____
_____
_____
_____
_____
_____
_____
_____
_____
_____
_____
_____
_____
_____
_____
_____
_____

Results:

	Unboiled seed plate A	Boiled seed plate B (control)
Iodine test (positive or negative) for starch agar plates		
Biuret test (positive or negative) for skimmed milk plates		

Diagram:

Risks:

_____
_____
_____
_____
_____

Risk management:

_____
_____
_____
_____

Skills:

_____
_____
_____
_____

Skill application:

_____
_____
_____
_____

Conclusions/comments:

_____
_____
_____
_____

Signature:

_____

Activity 22 Questions

1 Where in a seed is food stored?

2 Name a carbohydrate that you would expect to be present in this food store.

3 The broad bean is classified as a non-endospermic seed. What is a non-endospermic seed?

4 In this activity, why are the experimental seeds sterilised?

5 Why are the control seeds boiled?

6 Why is it recommended that blunt forceps are used for picking up the seeds?

7 What is agar?

8 What type of agar is used in this activity?

9 What aseptic techniques are used in this activity?

10 Why are these aseptic techniques used?

11 Why are the seeds incubated at 20°C for 2–3 days?

12 Why are the split seeds placed cut side down on the starch agar plates?

13 What causes the digestion of starch?

14 Give a reason why this experiment would be less likely to work in winter.

15 Describe and explain what happens to the control plate when iodine is added.

16 Describe and explain what happens to the experimental plate when iodine is added.

Examination note
This activity was examined in Section B of the Leaving Cert Biology Exam in **2009** (HL and OL) and **2006** (HL and OL).

Additional Experiment Work

Title: _____

_____ *Date:* _____

Procedure:

_____
_____
_____
_____
_____
_____
_____
_____
_____
_____
_____
_____
_____
_____
_____
_____
_____
_____

Results:

Diagram:

Risks:

Risk management:

Skills:

Skill application:

Conclusions/comments:

Signature:

Glossary

A

Abiotic factors – Non-living factors, e.g. soil type, light intensity, etc.

Active site – The part of an enzyme that comes in contact with the substrate upon which it acts.

Aerobic respiration – Respiration that requires the presence of oxygen.

Amylase – A digestive enzyme found in animals and plants that breaks down starch into maltose.

Anaerobic jar – A vessel that contains no oxygen.

Anaerobic respiration – Respiration that does not require the presence of oxygen.

Aorta – The blood vessel that carries oxygen-rich blood away from the heart.

Aseptic techniques – Techniques that aim to minimise the possibility of contamination with unwanted micro-organisms.

Atria – The upper chambers of the heart.

Auxins – A group of plant growth regulators (hormones).

B

Benedict's reagent – A blue liquid that turns red when heated in the presence of reducing sugar.

Biomolecule – A molecule found in living things.

Biuret reagent – A mixture of sodium hydroxide (clear) and copper sulfate (blue) that turns purple in the presence of protein.

Buffer – A chemical that keeps the pH of a solution fixed.

C

Calcium chloride – A chemical that, along with sodium alginate, forms a gel that immobilises yeast cells.

Catalase – An enzyme found in celery that speeds up the breakdown of hydrogen peroxide into water and oxygen.

Cell ultrastructure – The fine detail of a cell as viewed under an electron microscope.

Clinistix – Glucose testing strips that change colour depending on the concentration of glucose present.

Condenser – Part of a light microscope: it focuses light on to an object.

Constant – A factor that is kept the same during an experiment.

Control – An experiment that is set up so that the results of other experiments can be compared to it. (An experiment in which the variables are controlled so that the effects of varying one factor at a time may be observed.)

Coronary artery – The blood vessel that supplies the heart tissue with food and oxygen.

Cotyledon – Part of the plant embryo within the seed. Commonly known as the 'seed-leaf'.

D

Denatured enzyme – An enzyme whose shape has been irreversibly altered and so can no longer fit with its substrate.

Dermal tissue – The tissue that forms a protective layer on the outside of a plant. It consists of an outer waxy layer called the cuticle, and underneath is the epidermis.

Diaphragm – Part of a light microscope: it controls the amount of light reaching the object.

Dicot – A plant whose seed contains two cotyledons (seed leaves).

DNA – Deoxyribonucleic acid. Genetic material found in the nuclei of cells.

Dormancy – A period of time when seed growth and development are suspended until conditions become more favourable.

E

Elodea – An aquatic plant commonly known as Canadian pondweed.

Endosperm – A food storage area located within the seed surrounding the plant embryo.

Enzyme – A biological catalyst. A chemical that speeds up a reaction without being altered itself.

F

Fermentation – The process whereby yeast converts sugar into alcohol as they respire anaerobically.

Fermentation lock – A water-filled piece of glassware that attaches to a reaction vessel. It prevents gases entering the reaction vessel but allows them to leave.

G

Germination – The growth of a plant embryo within a seed.

Ground tissue – The tissue that makes up most of the inside of a plant. It may act as storage, support or photosynthetic tissue.

H

Hydrogen peroxide – A clear liquid that is broken down into water and oxygen by the enzyme catalase.

I

IAA – Indole acetic acid. A plant hormone belonging to the auxins group.

Identification key – Used in ecology fieldwork to help identify the organisms found.

Immobilisation – A technique whereby an enzyme or a cell is trapped so that it can be reused over and over again.

Iodine solution – A yellow-brown liquid that turns blue-black in the presence of starch.

Iodine stain – A yellow-brown liquid that is used to stain onion cells when viewing them under a light microscope.

Iodoform test – A chemical test for alcohol using sodium hypochlorite and potassium iodide and heat. The appearance of pale yellow crystals indicates a positive result.

L

Leaf yeast – A fungus found on the under surface of leaves.

Limewater – A clear liquid that turns cloudy in the presence of carbon dioxide.

M

Medulla oblongata – The region of the brain that measures the carbon dioxide level of the blood flowing through it and in turn helps regulate heart rate and breathing rate.

Methylene blue stain – A blue liquid that is used to stain human cheek cells when viewing them under a light microscope.

Monocot – A plant whose seed contains one cotyledon (seed leaf).

O

Osmosis – The movement of water molecules from an area of high water concentration to an area of low water concentration across a semi-permeable (selectively permeable) membrane.

P

Pacemaker – A region of nervous tissue found in the right atrium of the heart where electrical activity is generated.

Percentage cover – An estimate of the amount of ground in a quadrat covered by a named species.

Percentage frequency – The chance of finding a named species with any one throw of a quadrat.

Pericardium – The membrane that covers the outside of the heart.

pH – A measure of the acidity or basicity of a substance.

Phloem – Vascular tissue that transports food around plants.

Photosynthesis – The process whereby green plants make their own food (glucose) using carbon dioxide and water and give off oxygen as a by-product.

Product – The substance that is produced as a result of enzyme activity.

Protease (peptidase) enzyme – An enzyme that breaks down protein, e.g. trypsin, pepsin.

Pulmonary artery – The blood vessel that carries oxygen-poor blood from the heart to the lungs.

Pulmonary circulatory system – The part of the circulatory system that links the heart and the lungs.

Pulmonary vein – The blood vessel that carries oxygen-rich blood from the lungs to the heart.

Q

Qualitative study – A study that is carried out to determine whether or not an organism is present in an area.

Quantitative study – A study that is carried out to determine the number of organisms present in an area.

R

Reducing sugar – A type of sugar with an aldehyde group (e.g. glucose, maltose, lactose). *Note:* sucrose is not a reducing sugar.

Respiration – The release of energy from food.

S

Septum – The wall of muscle that separates the left and right sides of the heart.

Serial dilution – The stepwise dilution of a substance in solution where the dilution factor at each step is kept constant.

Sodium alginate – A chemical that, along with calcium chloride, forms a gel that immobilises yeast cells.

Sodium hydrogen carbonate ($NaHCO_3$) – A chemical that releases CO_2 when put in solution.

Sterile – An absence of all micro-organisms.

Substrate – The substance upon which an enzyme acts.

Systemic circulatory system – The part of the circulatory system that links the heart with the rest of the body.

T

Transverse section – A section formed by cutting through a specimen at right angles to its longitudinal axis.

V

Variable – A factor that is changed during an experiment.

Vascular tissue – The transport tissue in a plant consisting of xylem (transports water) and phloem (transports food).

Vena cava – The blood vessel that carries oxygen-poor blood back to the heart.

Ventricles – The lower chambers of the heart.

Visking tubing – An artificial semi-permeable (selectively permeable) membrane.

X

Xylem – Vascular tissue that carries water around plants.

Y

Yeast – A unicellular fungus that feeds on sugar and converts it into alcohol.